# Colorful Aircraft

Unique Paint Schemes on the World's Passenger Airliners

Norbert Andrup

**Schiffer Military History**
Atglen, PA

Interior Design: Norbert Andrup

Book translated by Dr. Edward Force

Copyright © 2010 by Schiffer Publishing, Ltd.
Library of Congress Control Number: 2010929864

Printed in China.
ISBN: 978-0-7643-3656-0

This book was originally published in German under the title
*Bunte Vögel* by Motorbuch-Verlag

We are interested in hearing from authors with book ideas on related topics.

Published by Schiffer Publishing Ltd.
4880 Lower Valley Road
Atglen, PA 19310
Phone: (610) 593-1777
FAX: (610) 593-2002
E-mail: Info@schifferbooks.com.
Visit our web site at: www.schifferbooks.com
Please write for a free catalog.
This book may be purchased from the publisher.
Please include $5.00 postage.
Try your bookstore first.

In Europe, Schiffer books are distributed by:
Bushwood Books
6 Marksbury Avenue
Kew Gardens
Surrey TW9 4JF
England
Phone: 44 (0) 20 8392-8585
FAX: 44 (0) 20 8392-9876
E-mail: Info@bushwoodbooks.co.uk.

# Contents

# Introduction

As well known as a colorful dog—almost everyone knows this saying. Colorful at any price is surely no recipe for success, but an eye-catching as well as tasteful design is, in any case, a successful advertisement. Yet it took an extremely long time before the idea of painting commercial airplanes in striking yet artistically valuable motifs caught on. For decades, into the fifties, commercial planes were used completely without paint, with shimmering metal, only window frames, logos, and lettering being painted. Since the beginning of the fifties the outsides of commercial aircraft gradually came to be painted white, particularly for climatic reasons. This was not very exciting.

In 1965 the avant-garde finally appeared thanks to the U.S. designer Alexander Girard. He was hired by the Tinker advertising agency to rework the appearance of the Braniff International Airways of Dallas radically—an airline that was strong, especially in the southern USA, and Latin America. His idea was not to paint his client's entire fleet with a single design, but to use a whole palette of colors. He found open doors and open ears at Braniff. Soon the colorful Braniff birds were known all over, a flying advertising campaign without words, and a perfect example of the beginning Pop-Art era, along with flowered miniskirts and shriekingly colorful bell-bottoms. At the end eight different colors were chosen; "the end of the plain plane," as Braniff accurately called it.

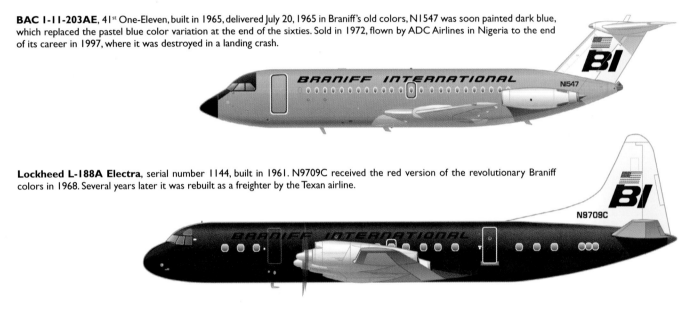

**BAC 1-11-203AE,** 41st One-Eleven, built in 1965, delivered July 20, 1965 in Braniff's old colors, N1547 was soon painted dark blue, which replaced the pastel blue color variation at the end of the sixties. Sold in 1972, flown by ADC Airlines in Nigeria to the end of its career in 1997, where it was destroyed in a landing crash.

**Lockheed L-188A Electra,** serial number 1144, built in 1961. N9709C received the red version of the revolutionary Braniff colors in 1968. Several years later it was rebuilt as a freighter by the Texan airline.

At the beginning of the seventies Braniff's formative concept was modified by the firm. The BAC 1-11, Boeing 707 and 727, Douglas DC-8, and Lockheed Electras were now two-tone, but no less strikingly colorful. There were four different versions of the "Flying Colors": red/gold, 2-tone blue, and 2-tone green and orange, the last reserved for the new Boeing 747.

**Boeing 727-62C,** 342nd 727, serial number 19245, built in 1966. First flew in the light blue version of the earliest bright colors, then in 1973 N7286 took on the green version of "flying colors." It remained with Braniff until 1981, then went to UPS, and was scrapped in 2003.

**Boeing 707-327C**, 507th 707, serial number 19107, built in 1966. Originally painted the ochre shade of the first colorful series, N7098 was painted in the red/gold version of the newly introduced "Flying Colors" at the end of 1971. Just a few months later, on July 1, 1972, the plane, used mainly for military charters, was sold.

In 1972 the advertising manager, George Gordon, had an idea. A fan of the world-famous artist Alexander Calder, best known for his mobiles, Gordon took a snow-white airplane model and flew to Calder in southern France. "I don't paint toys," was Calder's answer. But when Gordon repeated that he wanted to make the most unusual canvas of all time, a four-engine commercial airplane, available to Calder, the artist became excited: "A flying mobile, I like that." The first flying work of art was born. Calder painted several models, and Braniff decided which one they liked best. This design, called "Humor," was painted on a DC-8-62 and widely advertised.

**Douglas DC-8-62**, 3-4th DC-8, serial number 45899, built in 1967. N1805 first flew in mint green, and was painted in the green "Flying Colors" version (like the Boeing 727 opposite) in 1972. A year later, in 1973, it became a flying work of art. The Calder design remained on the plane until 1980; then it was painted terra-cotta brown (see next page).

**Boeing 727-291**, 549th 727, serial number 19993, built in 1968. After four years of service with Frontier Airlines, this plane was sold to Braniff on March 13, 1972, and registered N408BN. In 1975 it became the airline's second plane to be painted with a Calder design, and was repainted for the 200th anniversary of the USA in 1976. As already with the DC-8, the wings and power plants were included in the work of art. Shortly before his death in 1976, the renowned artist added a dragon-like serpent, which was painted on the no. 1 engine. Because of that, and also because this plane, for unexplained reasons, was hard to trim and had other problems, it was nicknamed "Sneaky Snake" by the Braniff crews. Naturally it was very unpopular with pilots. Yet N408BN remained in service until the airline went bankrupt in 1982. Then it flew for seven (!) other airlines until 1993. In that year it was blown up for the Holywood film "Bad Boys," somehow a fitting end for a special airplane.

**Boeing 747-127**, 100th 747, serial number 20207, built in 1970. Delivered January 5, 1971, the N601BN "Big Pumpkin" remained Braniff's only Jumbo-Jet for eight years, and bore a different color scheme from the rest of the fleet. In 1983 it finally became the last plane to fly for the original Braniff airline. Then it was sold to Tower Air, flew mainly military charters, and was taken out of service in 1992 after the first Gulf War.

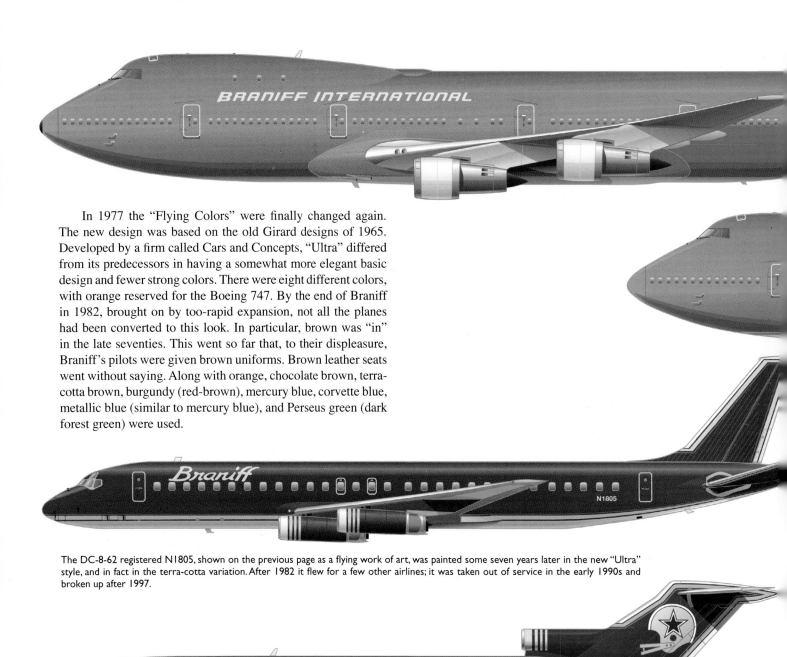

In 1977 the "Flying Colors" were finally changed again. The new design was based on the old Girard designs of 1965. Developed by a firm called Cars and Concepts, "Ultra" differed from its predecessors in having a somewhat more elegant basic design and fewer strong colors. There were eight different colors, with orange reserved for the Boeing 747. By the end of Braniff in 1982, brought on by too-rapid expansion, not all the planes had been converted to this look. In particular, brown was "in" in the late seventies. This went so far that, to their displeasure, Braniff's pilots were given brown uniforms. Brown leather seats went without saying. Along with orange, chocolate brown, terra-cotta brown, burgundy (red-brown), mercury blue, corvette blue, metallic blue (similar to mercury blue), and Perseus green (dark forest green) were used.

The DC-8-62 registered N1805, shown on the previous page as a flying work of art, was painted some seven years later in the new "Ultra" style, and in fact in the terra-cotta variation. After 1982 it flew for a few other airlines; it was taken out of service in the early 1990s and broken up after 1997.

**Boeing 727-227**, the 1353rd 727, serial number 21463, built in 1978. N457BN was delivered on June 13, 1978, in the mercury blue "Ultra" color. Shortly before Braniff's end it was given a special name as an advertisement for the Dallas Cowboys, the American football team located in Braniff's home town. But the plane was used for only two of the team's away games, which were both lost—no wonder, for dark blue was seen as an unlucky color by the players. After the airline's bankruptcy N457BN remained in the second Braniff fleet. Then it went to Federal Express as a freighter and received the number N481FE. It was finally retired in summer 2009.

**Boeing 747-SP27**, 405th 747, serial number 21785, built in 1979. Of the four 747SP planes intended for Asian routes, only three were briefly in service for Braniff. N603BN, delivered on October 30, 1979, was already given up the next January. In all, seven Jumbo Jets received the orange "Ultra" paint job; only the N601BN shown at left bore the "Braniff International" name, which differed in form from the "Braniff" name on most of the fleet. N603BN was also reequipped as a VIP plane in 1983-84 after its short tenure with Braniff, and delivered to Oman, where it still flies as A40-SO for the government, meaning the ruling family. It is perfectly maintained as before.

While Braniff was the definite protagonist among airlines in modern design and individual equipping, other airlines only slowly, and for a long time only in individual cases, accepted the idea of using an airplane as the carrier of a special message. Only the 200th anniversary of the USA in 1976 inspired other airlines to present something special, which usually did not go beyond large adhesive stickers. An exception was Overseas National, which presented two DC-8 planes in different red-white-blue Stars and Stripes designs. In 1977 Qantas decorated a Boeing 707 with Christmas greetings, while Trans Australia Airlines in 1980 portrayed the natural monument of Uluru (Ayers Rock).

**Boeing 707-338C**, 660th 707, serial number 19622, built in 1967. VH-EAB was delivered to Qantas on January 10, 1968, and baptized with the name "City of Canberra." In 1971 it was renamed "Winton" when the name of the capital city was given to the first Qantas 747. In 1977 VH-EAB was sold to the Belgian Young Cargo firm and the Qantas colors were painted over. A delivery delay of the 747 to replace the 707, though, compelled the airline to reactivate it briefly for the Christmas season, for which it received a special paint job. A few days after Christmas 1977 it finally left the fleet.

In the mid-seventies the Ecuadorean airline, Ecuatoriana, introduced a new, eye-catching color scheme: each plane in the fleet was given an individual, really wild paint job, in a mixed style of Indian patterns and the psychedelic style of the early seventies. After 1980 things were quiet for a long time in the airlines. Here and there large adhesive panels, usually concerning the opening of new routes, were applied, and that was essentially the situation until the early nineties. Braniff went bankrupt in 1983. While the new Braniff Airways firm was active, until it collapsed again five years after its predecessor, it used (partly) colorful "Ultra" designs, while elsewhere, as before, "uniform" colors were preferred. Thus before the 1990s, except for Braniff and Ecuatoriana, there were scarcely any colorful airplanes. The airlines were very concerned about expressing their corporate identity, even on their means of transit.

The honor of being the first real logo jet belongs to "Shamu One" of the successful U.S. low-price line Southwest Airlines, painted in the striking black-and-white logo of an orca whale in 1988.

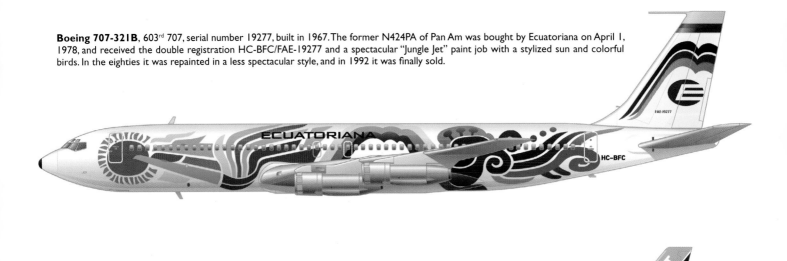

**Boeing 707-321B**, 603rd 707, serial number 19277, built in 1967. The former N424PA of Pan Am was bought by Ecuatoriana on April 1, 1978, and received the double registration HC-BFC/FAE-19277 and a spectacular "Jungle Jet" paint job with a stylized sun and colorful birds. In the eighties it was repainted in a less spectacular style, and in 1992 it was finally sold.

**Boeing 737-3H4**, 1549th 737, serial number 23938, built in 1988. This plane, registered N334SW, was put into service by Southwest Airlines on May 22, 1988. It was the first plane to be painted in the "Shamu" killer whale logo, which was later used on various other Boeing 737s of the Southwest Airlines fleet. Early in 2002 the paint was changed to the firm's new basic "canyon blue" color.

Better known internationally, in 1993, was the first Boeing 747 with the special "Marine Jumbo" logo of All Nippon Airways; interestingly, it was also inspired by a whale. The plane, though, that started the trend to special paint jobs more than any other, debuted in September 1994, and the logo is still in use 14 years later, though on a newer plane; The "Wunala Dreaming" of Qantas is doubtless the best-known advertising plane in the world. Shortly after this artistically dedicated and eye-catching bright red Boeing 747 appeared and became the ideal emissary of its land of origin, in turn airlines around the world discovered the advertising effect of a strikingly painted airliner. In 1994 the most colorful fleet in the world appeared in the form of the unfortunately short-lived Western Pacific Airlines, active only in the western USA. This airline rented out their planes to bear the advertising of other firms, and in this respect it was more influential than any other airline, which almost always used only single planes as flying placards. Almost every plane in their fleet, consisting almost exclusively of Boeing 737-300 planes, bore different advertising. But in 1998 these colorful birds disappeared from the skies when Western Pacific went bankrupt.

A further trend in special paint jobs, based on graphic art and pure commerce, also comes from the USA: photographic material on airplanes. The new firm Frontier Airlines introduced a color scheme in 1994 in which the scenes constituted of a kind of photo gallery. Animals from the western USA were depicted on each plane.

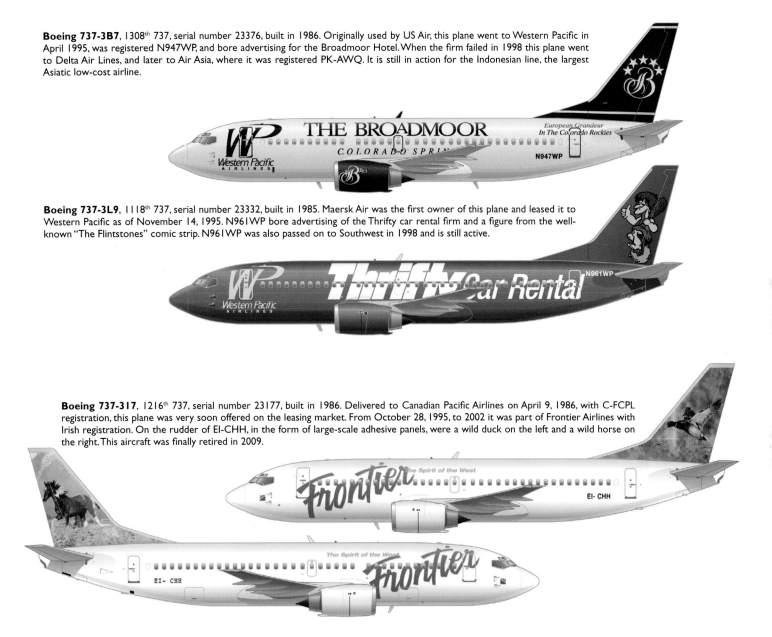

**Boeing 737-3B7**, 1308th 737, serial number 23376, built in 1986. Originally used by US Air, this plane went to Western Pacific in April 1995, was registered N947WP, and bore advertising for the Broadmoor Hotel. When the firm failed in 1998 this plane went to Delta Air Lines, and later to Air Asia, where it was registered PK-AWQ. It is still in action for the Indonesian line, the largest Asiatic low-cost airline.

**Boeing 737-3L9**, 1118th 737, serial number 23332, built in 1985. Maersk Air was the first owner of this plane and leased it to Western Pacific as of November 14, 1995. N961WP bore advertising of the Thrifty car rental firm and a figure from the well-known "The Flintstones" comic strip. N961WP was also passed on to Southwest in 1998 and is still active.

**Boeing 737-317**, 1216th 737, serial number 23177, built in 1986. Delivered to Canadian Pacific Airlines on April 9, 1986, with C-FCPL registration, this plane was very soon offered on the leasing market. From October 28, 1995, to 2002 it was part of Frontier Airlines with Irish registration. On the rudder of EI-CHH, in the form of large-scale adhesive panels, were a wild duck on the left and a wild horse on the right. This aircraft was finally retired in 2009.

Last but not least, a very unique area of special paintings can be mentioned that appeared at the end of the nineties for all kinds of anniversaries and has enjoyed ever-growing popularity: Retrojets, airplanes painted in more or less exactly imitated historical color schemes. The majority of larger or historically relevant airlines had or still have such a Retrojet or more in their fleet.

This brief outline is the beginning of the "colorful birds" story, extending into the 1990s. What has happened since then will be shown on the following 130 or more richly illustrated pages with aircraft of internationally flying airlines. For reasons of space companies only flying domestically have not been included. This book, on a purely visual theme, is not meant to be a scientific treatment of the history of flying advertisements. According to the saying that "one picture is worth a thousand words," most of the illustrations speak for themselves. With one exception all are side views to the same scale.

# Aerolineas Argentinas

Aerolineas Argentinas, the Argentine flag carrier, introduced essentially new color schemes in 1997, 2003, and in June 2010. The 1997 variant was done in the style of the Spanish Iberia airline, with which there was a close connection at the time, and that of 2003 was obviously based on that of Lufthansa. Special paintings by this airline are quite rare, and have appeared to date almost exclusively for sporting events.

**Boeing 747-287B**, 403rd 747, serial number 21938, built in 1979. LV-MLP was delivered to Aerolineas Argentinas on October 11, 1979. In 1997 this plane was given a paint job in Iberia style. It was decorated with soccer motifs for the 1998 soccer world championship in Frankfurt. At the end of 2006 it was taken out of service after having been leased for a time to Air Plus Comet.

**Boeing 747-287B**, 436th 747, serial number 21938, built in 1980. This plane, originally in service with Singapore Airlines with registration 9V-SQM, was leased by Aerolineas Argentinas in May 1998. LV-YPC bore a paint job identical, even to the colors of the engines, to the soccer world championship logo of LV-MLP. In October 2002 it was returned to the leaser and finally mothballed after a period in the service of Air Plus Comet.

**Boeing 737-287**, 387th 737, serial number 20966, built in 1974. LV-LIW, delivered on December 11, 1974, was given a simple special paint job in 1998 to advertise a telephone hot line. In February 2001 the veteran plane was taken out of fleet service.

**Boeing 747-287B**, 532nd 747, serial number 22592, built in 1981. LV-OOZ was turned over to Aerolineas Argentinas on August 26, 1981. To honor the Boca Juniors soccer team on its fifth victory in the South American championship it was given the "Pentacampeon" title in November 2003 and maintained as such until May 2004. In the same year, LV-OOZ was turned over to the Spanish sister airline Air Plus Comet, and was finally taken out of service in 2007.

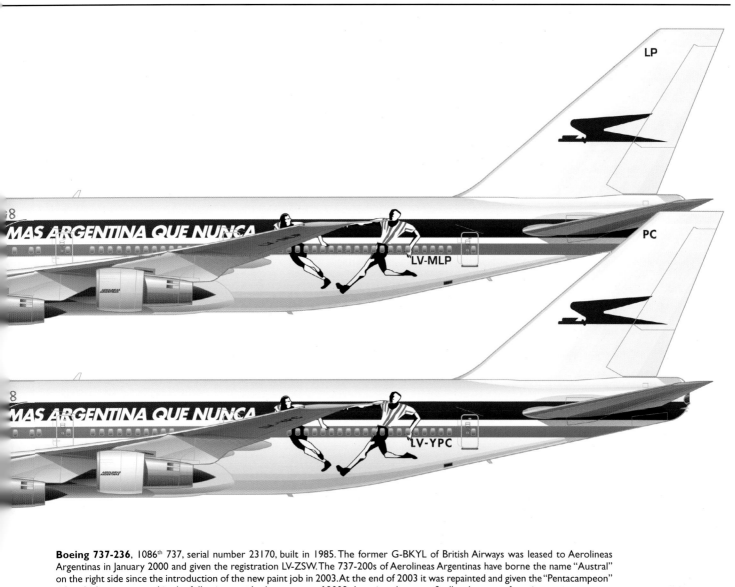

Boeing 737-236, 1086th 737, serial number 23170, built in 1985. The former G-BKYL of British Airways was leased to Aerolineas Argentinas in January 2000 and given the registration LV-ZSW. The 737-200s of Aerolineas Argentinas have borne the name "Austral" on the right side since the introduction of the new paint job in 2003. At the end of 2003 it was repainted and given the "Pentacampeon" title, which was removed in the following year. In the summer of 2008 the aging plane was finally taken out of service.

# AeroSur

The Bolivian AeroSur airline stands out because the paint job of every plane in its fleet differs from the others. Only the unusual turquoise-violet-white colors are common to all planes, with the exception of the new flagship aircraft, a single Boeing 747-400 introduced in 2009. The airline, which has grown in recent years at the cost of the suffering LAB state airline, uses older airliner models, like so many South American airlines, such as Boeing 727-200 and 737-200, though also a Boeing 757-200, a 767-200, and very recently several 747-300s. In 2008/2009 a Boeing 747-300 was used on the Madrid route, but this plane has since been replaced by a much newer 747-400; it is not only by far the largest, but also the most attractively painted plane of the fleet.

**Boeing 727-264**, 1676th 727, serial number 22409, built in 1980. This plane flew with registration XA-MEH in Mexicana service until 2004. In August 2004 it went to AeroSur, took on a Mexicana-based design with very different titles and logo from the rest of the fleet, and was registered CP-2447.

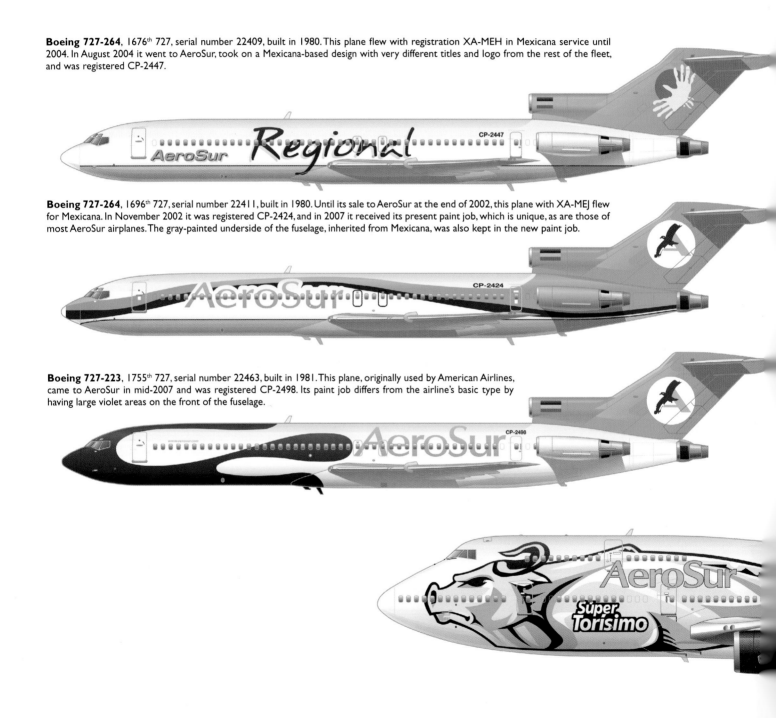

**Boeing 727-264**, 1696th 727, serial number 22411, built in 1980. Until its sale to AeroSur at the end of 2002, this plane with XA-MEJ flew for Mexicana. In November 2002 it was registered CP-2424, and in 2007 it received its present paint job, which is unique, as are those of most AeroSur airplanes. The gray-painted underside of the fuselage, inherited from Mexicana, was also kept in the new paint job.

**Boeing 727-223**, 1755th 727, serial number 22463, built in 1981. This plane, originally used by American Airlines, came to AeroSur in mid-2007 and was registered CP-2498. Its paint job differs from the airline's basic type by having large violet areas on the front of the fuselage.

**Boeing 727-222**, 1528th 727, serial number 21904, built in 1979. The former N7450U of United Air Lines had been taken out of service in 2001, then flew from 2002 to 2008 for Pan American Airways, where it was registered N346PA. At the end of 2008 the old but still-elegant plane came to AeroSur as CP-2515. It too bears an individual paint job.

**Boeing 737-281**, 586th 737, serial number 21768, built in 1979. On July 12, 1979, it was delivered to All Nippon Airways with registration JA8454, and the aging 737 came to AeroSur on November 3, 2006. The nose of the plane, now registered CP-2484, was painted with the airline's own cartoon character "Aerosurito."

**Boeing 737-281**, 594th 737, serial number 21771, built in 1979. The original owner, All Nippon Airways, received it with JA 8454 registration on July 12, 1979. In 2006 the 737 was leased to AeroSur and registered CP-2476. At the end of 2007 this plane, after flying with a simpler paint job, was painted in individual style.

**Boeing 747-443**, 1275th 747, serial number 32339, built in 2001. Originally destined for Alitalia (that is why it is having that airline´s designator „43") this aircraft belonging to GE Capital was instead delivered to Virgin Atlantic Airways in May 2001. Carrying the registration G-VROM until it was leased to Aerosur in November 2009, it was then reregistered CP-2603 and painted in a stunning livery called „Super Torisimo", replacing the aging and similarly, but simpler painted „Torisimo", the first 747 of Aerosur.

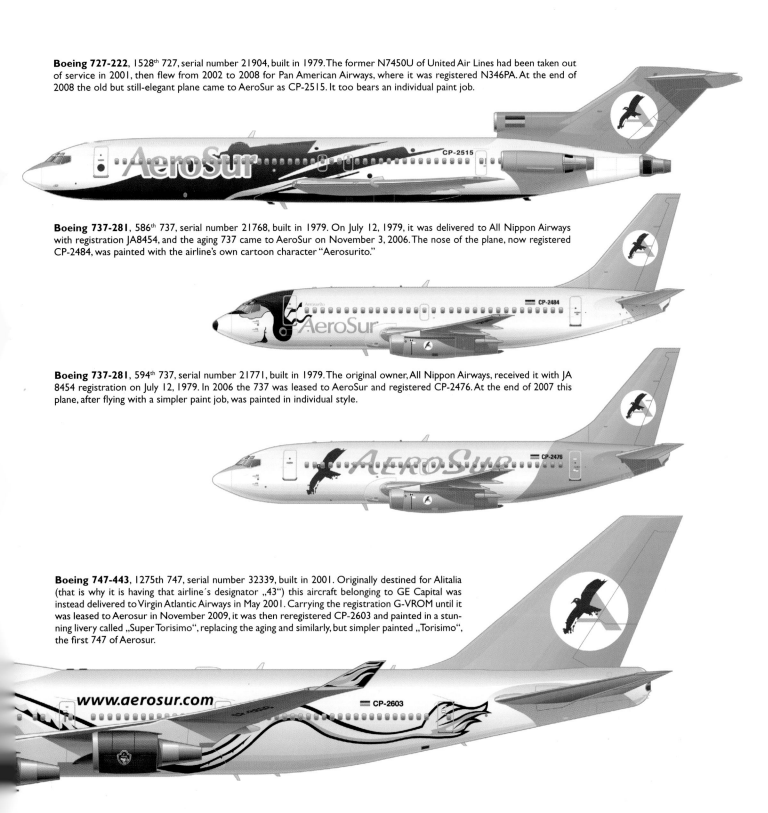

# Air Asia

This Malayan airline, flying since 1996 and having become Asia's largest low-cost airline, is, along with its Thai and Indonesian sister lines, one of the world's most colorful airlines. Scarcely any plane in the fleet is identical with its neighbors, and many bear advertising, since the airline reinvented itself in 2003 and replaced its original blue and green colors with a more dynamic red. Since 2007 the aging, pre-owned Boeing 737s have been replaced or joined by new Airbus A320s; since the end of 2007 Airbus A330s and A340s have also been added.

**Boeing 737-301**, 1248th 737, serial number 23510, built in 1986. This plane, delivered to Piedmont Airlines on July 9, 1986, with registration N321P, came from US Air in the autumn of 2003. The 9M-AAI was painted in the design of the Malaysian flag and named "Jamur Gemilang." Passed on to the Thai sister line in July 2007 and registered HS-AAI, it was also given a special paint job there, a design of the Thai national tourist office.

**Boeing 737-3L9**, 1402nd 737, serial number 23718, built in 1987. Air Asia's 9M-AAB had been delivered to Maersk Air as OY-MMN on June 26, 1987. Sold at the end of 2004, the plane was given a new paint job shortly thereafter, celebrating the line's award as the best regional airline in 2003. By mid-2006 pictures of collaborators were seen on the fuselage.

**Boeing 737-3B7**, 1339th 737, serial number 23378, built in 1987, Air Asia, 9M-AAU. Delivered to US Air as N327AU on February 9, 1987, it was later in service with Western Pacific and Delta Air Lines. It was leased for two years by Air Asia as of November 1, 2005, and given a special paint job with the logo of the Thai solar module manufacturer Solartron. In May 2008 the aging 737 was leased to the Mexican low-cost carrier Viva Aerobus.

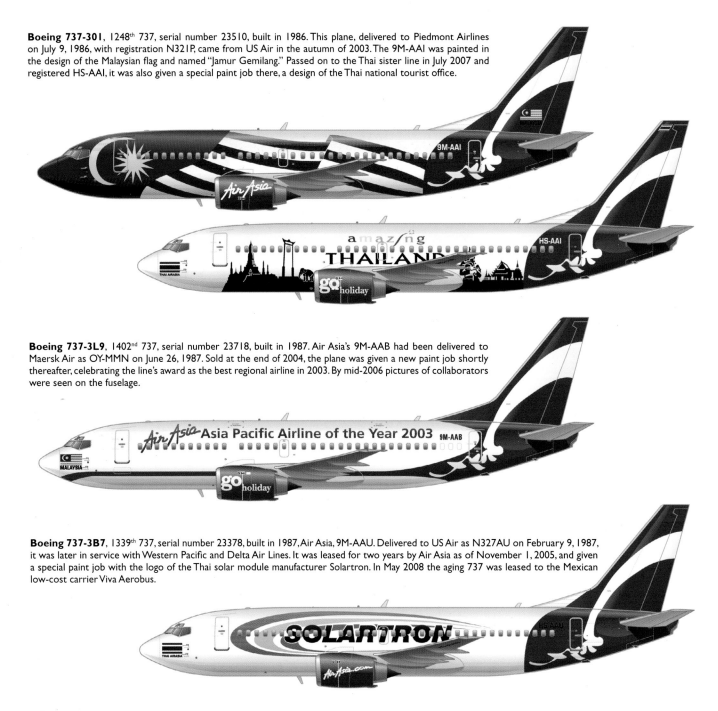

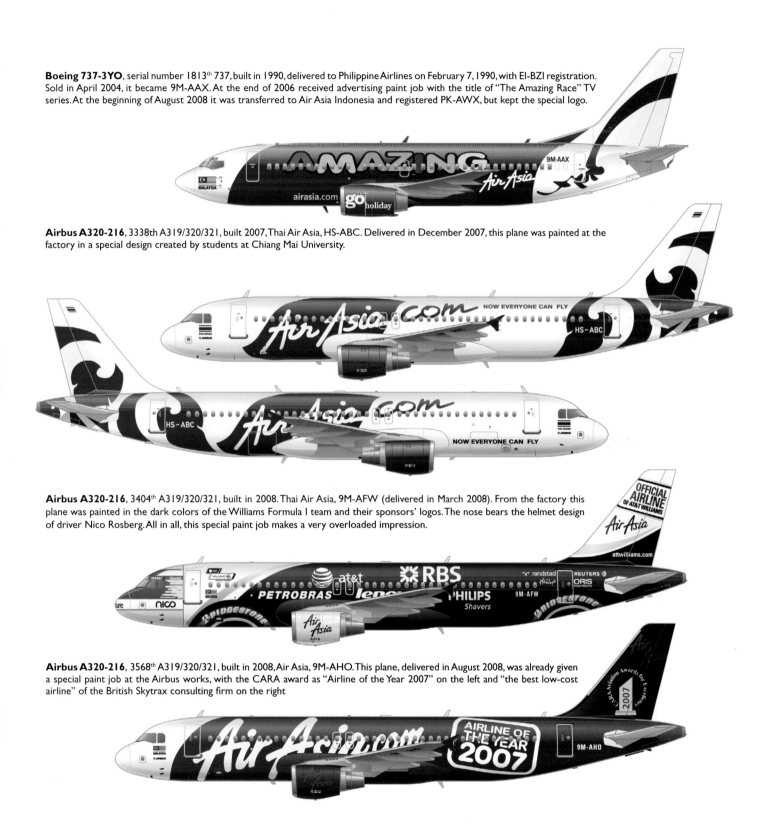

**Boeing 737-3YO**, serial number 1813th 737, built in 1990, delivered to Philippine Airlines on February 7, 1990, with EI-BZI registration. Sold in April 2004, it became 9M-AAX. At the end of 2006 received advertising paint job with the title of "The Amazing Race" TV series. At the beginning of August 2008 it was transferred to Air Asia Indonesia and registered PK-AWX, but kept the special logo.

**Airbus A320-216**, 3338th A319/320/321, built 2007, Thai Air Asia, HS-ABC. Delivered in December 2007, this plane was painted at the factory in a special design created by students at Chiang Mai University.

**Airbus A320-216**, 3404th A319/320/321, built in 2008. Thai Air Asia, 9M-AFW (delivered in March 2008). From the factory this plane was painted in the dark colors of the Williams Formula 1 team and their sponsors' logos. The nose bears the helmet design of driver Nico Rosberg. All in all, this special paint job makes a very overloaded impression.

**Airbus A320-216**, 3568th A319/320/321, built in 2008, Air Asia, 9M-AHO. This plane, delivered in August 2008, was already given a special paint job at the Airbus works, with the CARA award as "Airline of the Year 2007" on the left and "the best low-cost airline" of the British Skytrax consulting firm on the right

# Air Atlanta Icelandic

Air Atlanta Icelandic is a charter carrier and leasing firm founded in 1986. Originally it had Boeing 707s and Lockheed Tristars, but since the mid-nineties it has obtained a number of mostly older Boeing 747s, and carries out a number of airline services under contract; for example, Hadj Flights for Garuda Indonesia or Saudi Arabian Airlines. Despite the often exotic services, notable special paint jobs have remained rare.

**Boeing 747-246B**, 137th 747, serial number 19825, built in 1971. This plane, originally flying for Japan Airlines with JA8106 registration, was bought by Air Atlanta in December 1999 and registered TF-ATF. In 2002 it bore a special logo for a display at the air travel festival in Oshkosh, Wisconsin. In 2003 it was mothballed after 32 years of service.

**Boeing 747-243B**, 618th 747, serial number 23301, built in 1985. Delivered to Alitalia on July 24, 1985, and flying with I-DEMV registration, this Jumbo-Jet was leased to Air Atlanta in January 2004. With the new registration TF-ARO, it was selected in June 2004 to bring the Olympic flame to Athens and was given an elaborate special design in the form of large adhesive panels, which were removed just a month later. The plane was taken out of service in 2006.

**Airbus A320-211**, 159th A320, built in 1991. C-FFWN received a special paint job in 2002 for the airline's 65th anniversary. Although two planes are now flying with special paint jobs for the 70th anniversary, this Airbus still bears the bright red logo with the old title as of early 2009.

Air Canada remains as Canada's only important international airline. To date, individual planes of various sizes have received special paint jobs. Whether for anniversaries, important sporting events, or other occasions, no basic pattern can be observed, as the designs are so varied.

**Boeing 767-38E ER**, 411th 767, serial number 25404, built in 1991. Delivered to Asiana on January 24, 1992, it flew as HL 7267, mainly on regional routes in Asia, before moving to Canadian Airlines, and then to Air Canada in May 2001. There the plane, now registered C-GBZR, was given a special "Free Spirit" paint job. In 2007 the rudder was given a new ice blue and red design, but the special painting of the fuselage was kept.

**Boeing 767-375 ER**, 216th 767, serial number 24083, built in 1988. C-FCAE, delivered on May 3, 1988, flew 13 years for Canadian Airlines, until its first owner merged with Air Canada on April 1, 2001. In 2007 it was painted in the new ice blue color, but with a different fuselage pattern that referred to the 70th anniversary of the founding of the ancestor line, Trans-Canada Airlines. The A321 C-GIUB was given the same anniversary design.

# Air China

The most important international airline from the People's Republic of China naturally prepared four airplanes with various special designs as advertising for the 2008 Olympic Games in Peking. This began at the end of 2005 with a factory-new Boeing 737-700, and a year later came two 737-800s. At the beginning of 2008 the "flagship" of the Olympic fleet, an A330-200, appeared.

**Airbus A330-243**, 785th A330/340, built in 2006. B-6075, delivered in November 2006, had the honor of transporting the Olympic flame to China, for which it received an attractive special paint job in the colors of the Chinese Olympic team at the beginning of 2008. In October 2008 that logo was replaced by a new red-gold color scheme.

**Boeing 737-86N**, 2096th 737NG, serial number 34258, built in 2006. In November 2006 B-5176 was delivered to Air China. It bears a special design with the mascots of the 2008 Olympic Games in Peking. The sister plane B-5178 bears the identical paint job.

# Air China

Through the 2008 Olympics Air China obviously got into the spirit, for within the first six months after the games four new special paint jobs appeared in short order: two A330s, one A320, and one 777-200.

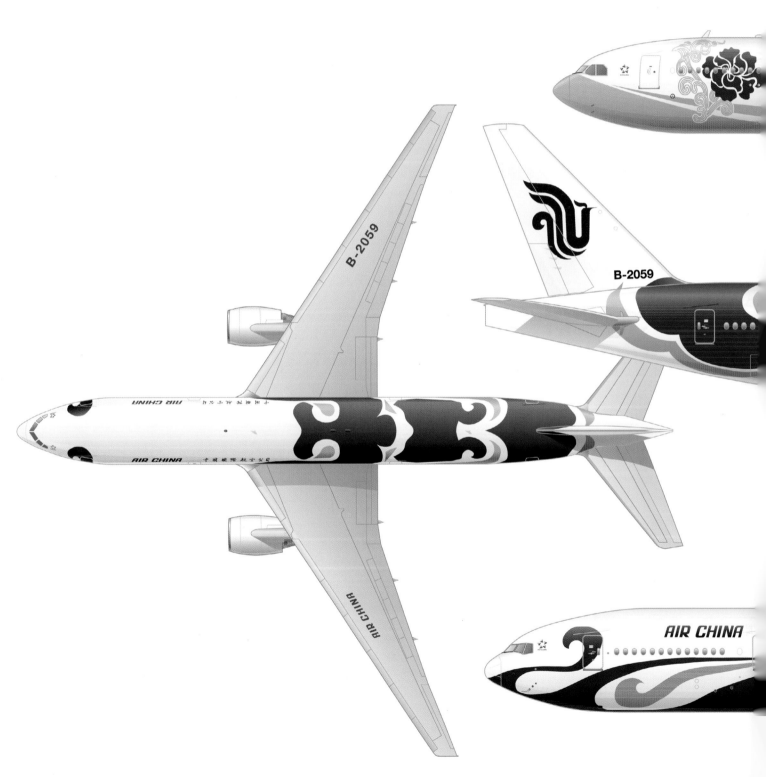

**Airbus A330-243**, 785th A330/340, built in 2006. B-6076, delivered in 2006, was the sister plane to the B-6075 shown on the previous pages, and also received a special paint job in the autumn of 2008, with blue instead of red but the identical graphics.

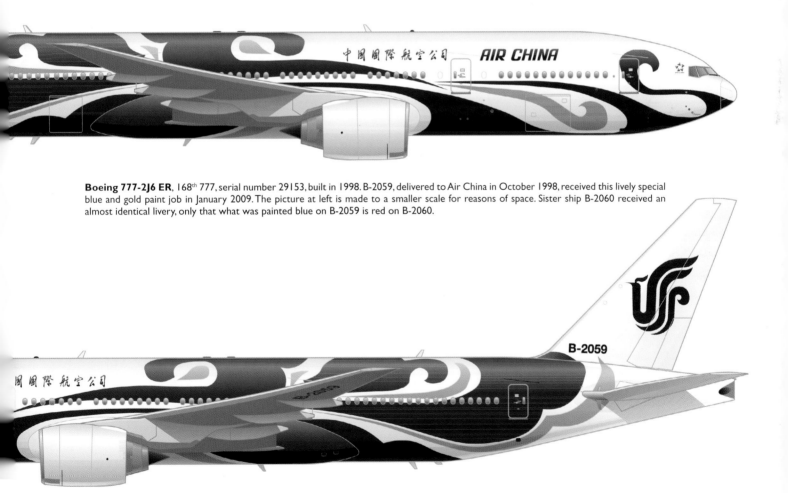

**Boeing 777-2J6 ER**, 168th 777, serial number 29153, built in 1998. B-2059, delivered to Air China in October 1998, received this lively special blue and gold paint job in January 2009. The picture at left is made to a smaller scale for reasons of space. Sister ship B-2060 received an almost identical livery, only that what was painted blue on B-2059 is red on B-2060.

# Air France

Fifteen years after they introduced their truly revolutionary logo in the 1970s, Air France decided it was time to change this design, at least in details. Since the logo turned out to be very sensitive to dust they tried gray paint on the underside and various blue and silver stripes above. Fortunately none of these attempts suited the executives, and so Air France planes still fly around the earth with snow-white paint, as before.

**Boeing 747-228B Combi,** 364th 747, serial number 21731, built in 1979. F-BPVX was delivered on March 28, 1979. In 1992 it was one of the planes on which experimental designs were tried. It was taken out of service in 2003 and broken up at Chalons-Vatry.

**Boeing 747-228B Combi,** 503rd 747, serial number 2242B, built in 1980. It was delivered with American registration N1305E on March 25, 1981. Six years later it finally was given the French registration F-GCBD. In 1992 it briefly bore experimental paint. Rebuilt as a freighter in 1997, it flew with Air France until the end of 2007. In 2008 it went to the newly founded French Global Airlines, a branch of the former MK Airlines, only to be retired in the spring of 2009.

**Boeing 747-428,** 889th 747, serial number 25334. Delivered on December 9, 1991, the factory-new F-GITC was immediately chosen for the small test-paint fleet. In 1993 it was given standard paint again.

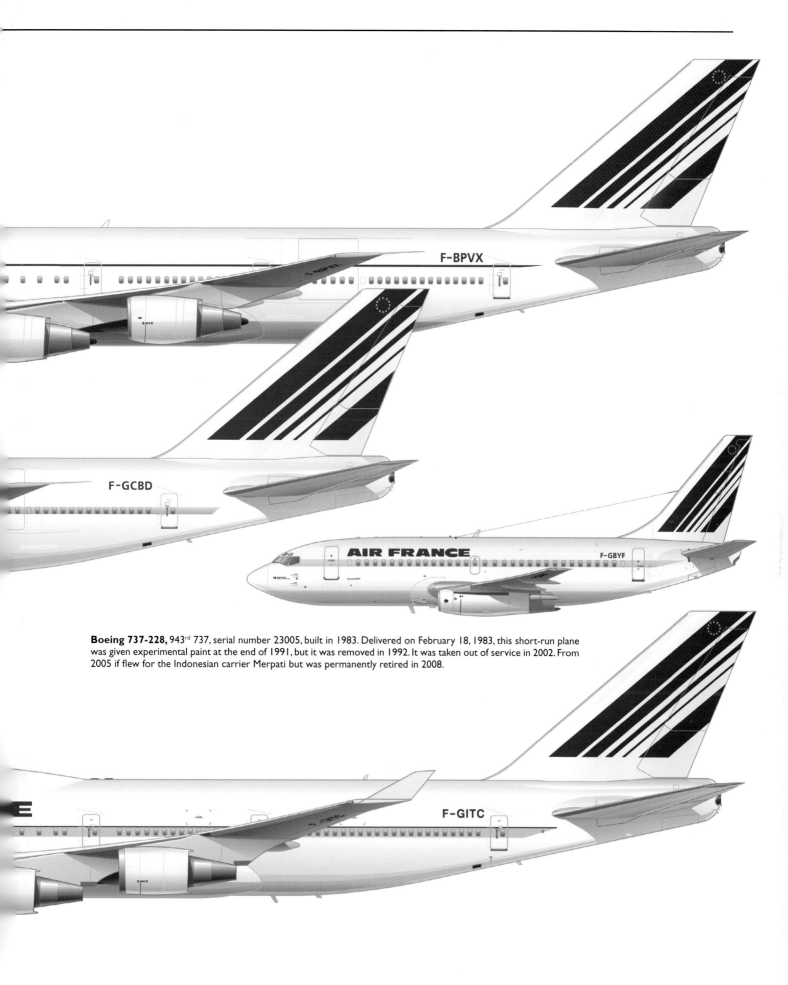

**AIR FRANCE**

F-BPVX

F-GCBD

F-GBYF

F-GITC

**Boeing 737-228,** 943rd 737, serial number 23005, built in 1983. Delivered on February 18, 1983, this short-run plane was given experimental paint at the end of 1991, but it was removed in 1992. It was taken out of service in 2002. From 2005 if flew for the Indonesian carrier Merpati but was permanently retired in 2008.

# Air France

The greatest event in France in the nineties, the soccer world championship of 1998, was also celebrated suitably by Air France. On that occasion a large number of Air France planes were given a special logo, each with a player on the rear half of the fuselage in the jersey of a participating nation.

When possible, planes with the colors of a particular country were assigned to fly to that country. After that there were no new types coming from Paris for ten years until, at the end of 2008, one A320 was given a retro paint job to commemorate the firm's 75th anniversary.

**Boeing 747-128,** 227th 747, serial number 20799, built in 1973. Delivered to Air France on December 21, 1991, this jumbo first flew with American N63305 registration; in 1982 it was given French F-BPVM registration. In 1998 it was given a special paint job for the world soccer championship. On the left side was a player in the USA uniform, on the right a Mexican. In March 2000 F-BPVM's service ended. With numerous other old Air France planes it was taken to Chateauroux, where it was broken up shortly afterward.

**List of planes with soccer world championship paint jobs. Illustrated players listed for the left side, then for right.**
B747-4B3 (F-GEXA), Japan, Argentina. B747-3B3 (F-GETA), Jamaica, Paraguay. B 747-128 (F-BPVM), USA, Mexico.
A340-313 (F-GLZX), Brazil, Colombia. A340-313 (F-GLZL), South Korea, South Africa.
A310-203 (F-GEMD), Nigeria, Saudi Arabia.
A320-211 (F-GFKM), Germany, Norway. A320-211 (F-GFKU), Italy, Holland. A320-211 (F-GFKH), Yugoslavia, Bulgaria. A320-211 (F-GJVA), Spain, Austria. A320-211 (F-GHQC), France, Scotland. A320-111 (F-GGEA), Tunisia, Morocco. A320-111 (F-GGEF), Iran, Denmark. A320-211 (F-GHQE), Cameroon, Belgium. A320-211 (F-GHQF), Croatia, Chile. A320-211 (F-GFKO), Romania, Britain.

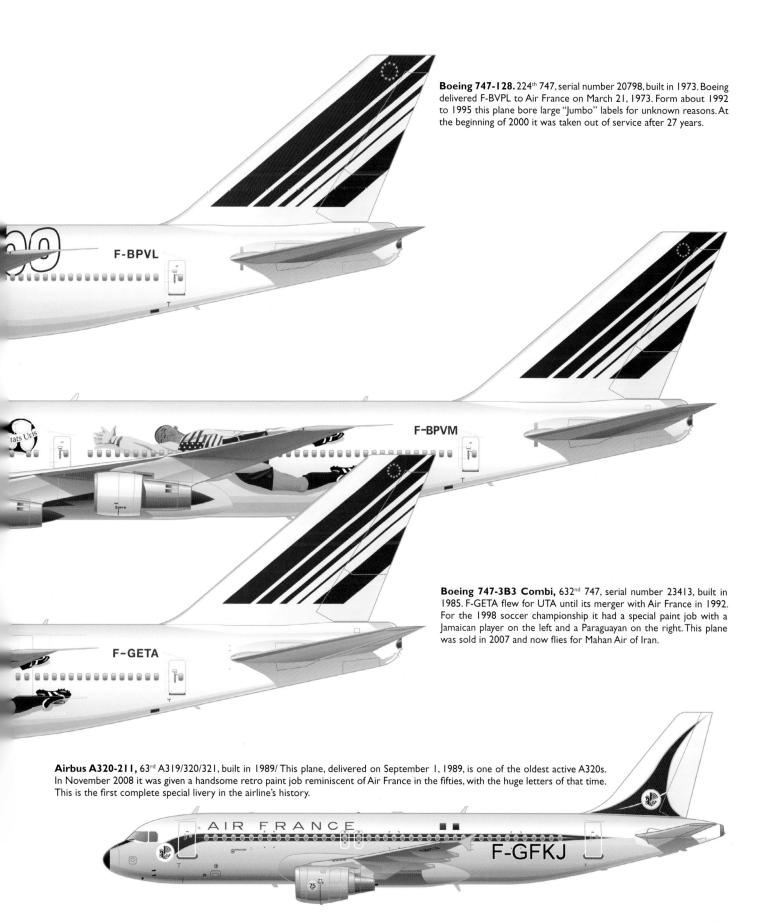

**Boeing 747-128.** 224th 747, serial number 20798, built in 1973. Boeing delivered F-BVPL to Air France on March 21, 1973. Form about 1992 to 1995 this plane bore large "Jumbo" labels for unknown reasons. At the beginning of 2000 it was taken out of service after 27 years.

F-BPVL

F-BPVM

**Boeing 747-3B3 Combi,** 632nd 747, serial number 23413, built in 1985. F-GETA flew for UTA until its merger with Air France in 1992. For the 1998 soccer championship it had a special paint job with a Jamaican player on the left and a Paraguayan on the right. This plane was sold in 2007 and now flies for Mahan Air of Iran.

F-GETA

**Airbus A320-211,** 63rd A319/320/321, built in 1989/ This plane, delivered on September 1, 1989, is one of the oldest active A320s. In November 2008 it was given a handsome retro paint job reminiscent of Air France in the fifties, with the huge letters of that time. This is the first complete special livery in the airline's history.

AIR FRANCE

F-GFKJ

# Air New Zealand

New Zealand's international airline is one of the flight firms that have recognized the advertising effect of colorful and interesting paint jobs and uses them regularly. The best known were probably the Boeing 747-400, 767-300, and Airbus A320 that from the end of 2002 to 2004 bore various motifs from the film trilogy "Lord of the Rings," produced in New Zealand, around the world. The lesser-known other colorful jets of Air NZ can be seen here.

**Boeing 737-219C,** 928th 737, serial number 22994, built in 1982. This "Piopio," as ZK-NQC was called, was delivered to Air New Zealand on December 2, 1982. At the same time as the 747 shown above and a Saab 340, this 737 had large "All-Blacks" label applied at the end of 1999 to honor the national rugby team. The venerable plane still flew for Air New Zealand until the beginning of 2001.

**Boeing 737-33R,** 2975th 737, serial number 28873, built in 1997. Delivered on January 9, 1998, ZK-NGA bore a special logo from the start for the millennium, which was also advertising for the America's Cup races that took place off Auckland in 2000. At the beginning of 2001 this special logo was removed. The plane now flies for Estonian Air with ES-ABJ registration.

**Boeing 747-419,** 1228th 747, serial number 29375, built in 1999. ZK-NBW was delivered on September 8, 1999, and immediately given, for a few months, a special logo to honor the New Zealand national rugby team, the All-Blacks, as they took part in the world championship.

ZK-NBW

holidays

ZK-FRE

**Boeing 737-3U3,** 2992nd 737, serial number 28742, built in 1998. This plane was in use by the short-lived U.S. Pronair line, and then by Freedom Air, before it was leased to Air New Zealand with ZK-FRE registration. In 2007 it was given a special logo to advertise regional vacation flights.

ZK-FRE

holidays

# Alitalia

The Italian flag carrier Alitalia had three planes in attractive advertising logos, including two Jumbo-Jets, in use around 2000. Why this policy was halted by the chronically financially troubled airline is unfortunately not known.

**McDonnell Douglas DC-9-82 (MD-82),** 1737th DC-9, serial number 49970, built in 1990. I-DAVZ was delivered to Alitalia on July 31, 1990, and named "Brescia," but leased to ATI. On October 30, 1994, ATI was merged with Alitalia. In March 2000 I-DAVZ was given an advertising logo for the fast food McDonalds™ chain; alas, it was not as successful as the other two advertising Jumbo-Jets of the same time. Since the end of 2001 the plane flew with a standard logo. It was taken out of service in December 2008.

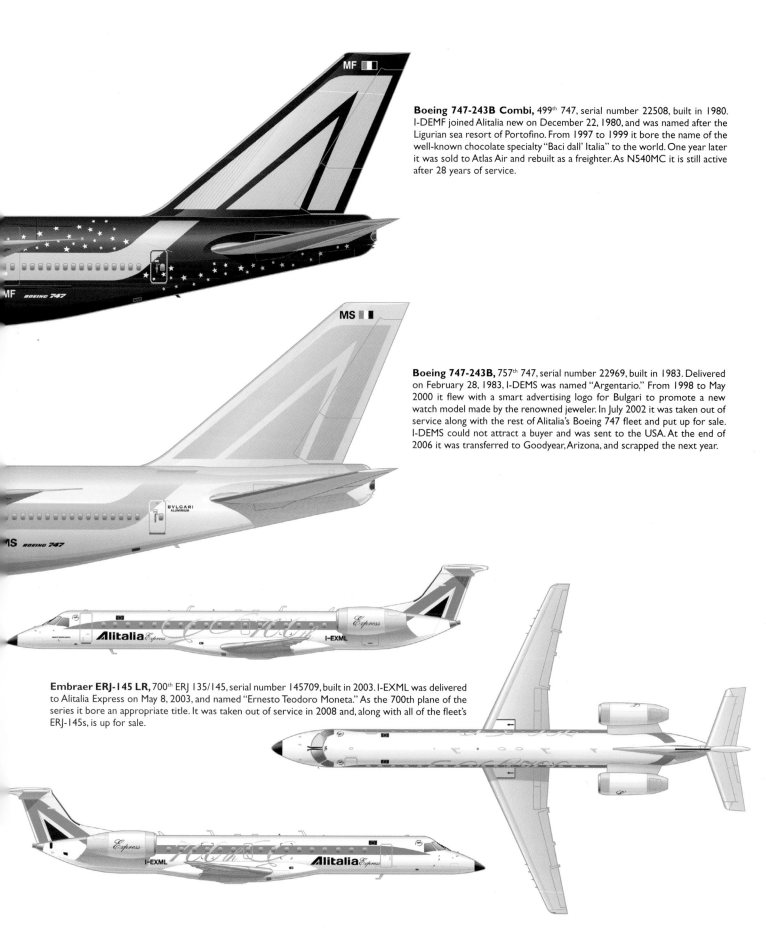

**Boeing 747-243B Combi,** 499th 747, serial number 22508, built in 1980. I-DEMF joined Alitalia new on December 22, 1980, and was named after the Ligurian sea resort of Portofino. From 1997 to 1999 it bore the name of the well-known chocolate specialty "Baci dall' Italia" to the world. One year later it was sold to Atlas Air and rebuilt as a freighter. As N540MC it is still active after 28 years of service.

**Boeing 747-243B,** 757th 747, serial number 22969, built in 1983. Delivered on February 28, 1983, I-DEMS was named "Argentario." From 1998 to May 2000 it flew with a smart advertising logo for Bulgari to promote a new watch model made by the renowned jeweler. In July 2002 it was taken out of service along with the rest of Alitalia's Boeing 747 fleet and put up for sale. I-DEMS could not attract a buyer and was sent to the USA. At the end of 2006 it was transferred to Goodyear, Arizona, and scrapped the next year.

**Embraer ERJ-145 LR,** 700th ERJ 135/145, serial number 145709, built in 2003. I-EXML was delivered to Alitalia Express on May 8, 2003, and named "Ernesto Teodoro Moneta." As the 700th plane of the series it bore an appropriate title. It was taken out of service in 2008 and, along with all of the fleet's ERJ-145s, is up for sale.

# American Airlines

American Airlines is one of the four remaining major U.S. airlines. The line's logo, in metallic silver with red-white-blue trim, is one of the oldest in air travel, and surely the oldest among internationally operating lines. Changes have to be made to keep up with the "plastic" planes of the coming decade, such as the Boeing 787 and Airbus A350, for polished aluminum is no longer available. The first AA special logo debuted in 1999 with a so-called Retrojet, the Boeing 757-200 in fifties paint. The airline, after the mergers of Delta/NWA and United/Continental, is only the no. 3 airline in the U.S., but still has used few specially painted planes. American Airlines, with a fleet numbering over 600 planes, surprisingly does not use any very large planes, since it does not offer enough routes that it feels would justify the use of the Boeing 747 or Airbus A380.

**Boeing 757-223,** 842nd 757, serial number 29589, built in 1998. N679AN was delivered to American Airlines on January 15, 1999, and already bore the retro painting for the firm's 70th anniversary. Since mid-2003 it has flown with the usual standard logo.

**Boeing 737-823,** 720th 737NG, serial number 29538, built in 2000. After the retro paint job on the 757 shown above had gone over well with the public, American Airlines decided shortly thereafter to give another plane a historic logo. N915AA, delivered new on December 12, 2000, has flown since then with the "Astrojet" paint of the sixties. It was fitted with winglets in 2007.

**Embraer ERJ145,** 860th ERJ-135/145, serial number 145860, built in 2005. N691AE was transferred to the regional branch firm of American Eagle in 2005. Unlike the shimmering metallic planes of the main fleet, the smaller American Eagle planes are painted white. Along with the fleet's largest plane, it, the fleet's smallest plane, has borne since 2008 the pink stripe of the Sarah J. Komen Initiative for breast cancer care.

Austrian Airlines, founded at the end of 1957 and bought up by Lufthansa in December 2008, had in its 100-plane fleet several planes with special paint jobs. Some flew and still fly in the Star Alliance look; otherwise, and not surprisingly, music was a main theme. In the Mozart Year of 2006 an A340 flew for the Vienna Philharmonic, an A320 completely in a Mozart design. Shortly afterward two smaller jets were given special logos to advertise the European world championship that took place in Austria, and one A320 was given retro paint for the airline's 50th anniversary.

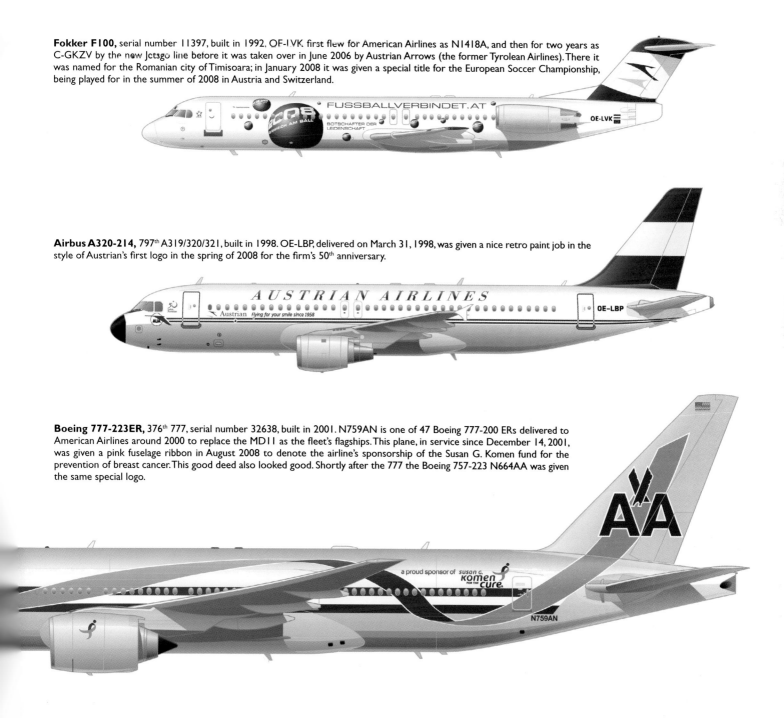

**Fokker F100,** serial number 11397, built in 1992. OF-IVK first flew for American Airlines as N1418A, and then for two years as C-GKZV by the now Jetsgo line before it was taken over in June 2006 by Austrian Arrows (the former Tyrolean Airlines). There it was named for the Romanian city of Timisoara; in January 2008 it was given a special title for the European Soccer Championship, being played for in the summer of 2008 in Austria and Switzerland.

**Airbus A320-214,** 797th A319/320/321, built in 1998. OE-LBP, delivered on March 31, 1998, was given a nice retro paint job in the style of Austrian's first logo in the spring of 2008 for the firm's 50th anniversary.

**Boeing 777-223ER,** 376th 777, serial number 32638, built in 2001. N759AN is one of 47 Boeing 777-200 ERs delivered to American Airlines around 2000 to replace the MD11 as the fleet's flagships. This plane, in service since December 14, 2001, was given a pink fuselage ribbon in August 2008 to denote the airline's sponsorship of the Susan G. Komen fund for the prevention of breast cancer. This good deed also looked good. Shortly after the 777 the Boeing 757-223 N664AA was given the same special logo.

# ANA All Nippon Airways

All Nippon Airways, ANA for short, is typical of Japanese airlines. In no other country are there so many "colorful birds." Two ANA jets started it, influencing the modern trend toward specially-painted passenger airliners very decisively: the "Marine Jumbo" and "Marine Jumbo Junior" shown here. Only after these two planes did the style of special liveries really catch on. The left and right sides of all ANA special paint jobs have been formed differently.

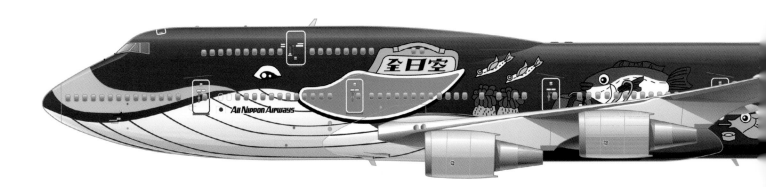

**Boeing 767-381**, 520th 767, 25659, built in 1993, All Nippon Airways JA8579, delivered December 1, 1993. Shortly after the "Marine Jumbo" had been so successful the brand new "Marine Jumbo Junior" was unveiled. The 767, though, flew in this livery for only two years.

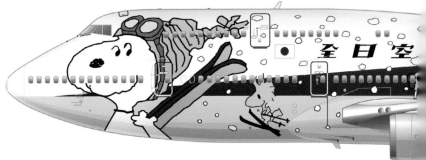

**Boeing 747-481D**, 1060th 747, serial number 27436, built in 1995. The All Nippon Airways JA8965 was delivered on April 24, 1995. This short-flight Jumbo was the second plane in "Snoopy" paint from the summer of 1997 to 1998. The sister plane JA 8961 bore a somewhat different "Snoopy" paint job at the same time.

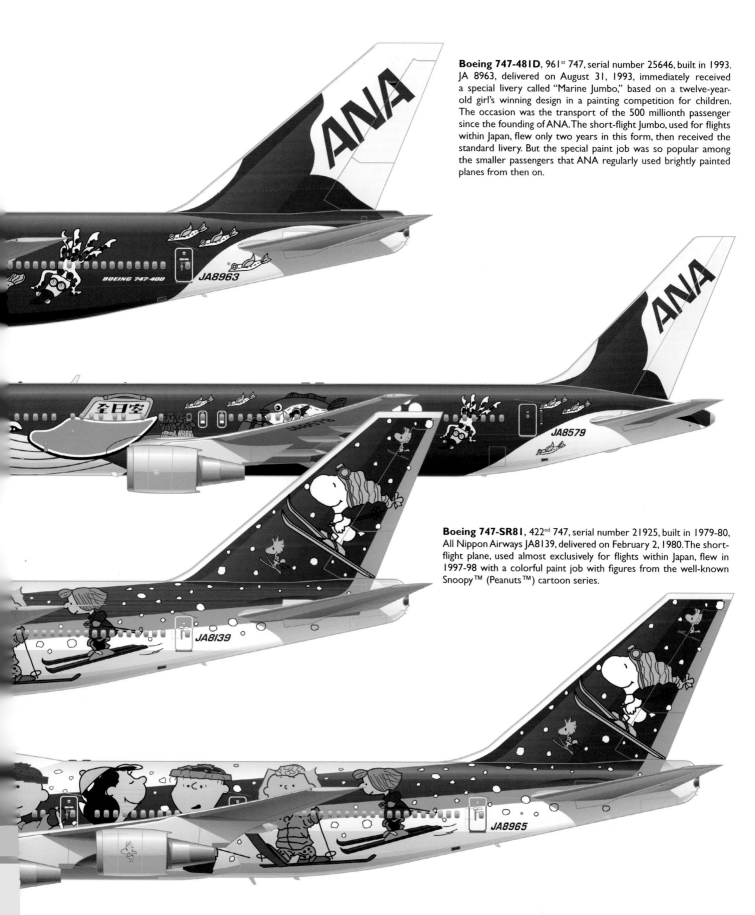

**Boeing 747-481D**, 961st 747, serial number 25646, built in 1993. JA 8963, delivered on August 31, 1993, immediately received a special livery called "Marine Jumbo," based on a twelve-year-old girl's winning design in a painting competition for children. The occasion was the transport of the 500 millionth passenger since the founding of ANA. The short-flight Jumbo, used for flights within Japan, flew only two years in this form, then received the standard livery. But the special paint job was so popular among the smaller passengers that ANA regularly used brightly painted planes from then on.

**Boeing 747-SR81**, 422nd 747, serial number 21925, built in 1979-80, All Nippon Airways JA8139, delivered on February 2, 1980. The short-flight plane, used almost exclusively for flights within Japan, flew in 1997-98 with a colorful paint job with figures from the well-known Snoopy™ (Peanuts™) cartoon series.

# ANA All Nippon Airways

Typical of Japanese airlines, and of ANA in particular, is that the special paint jobs of their planes are intended to speak to children above all. Again and again, Boeing 747s have been chosen to bear cartoon motifs to address the parents through the children of their customers. The Japanese Pokemon™ (Pocket Monster) characters enjoy particularly great popularity. Most of the planes decorated in this way have been short-flight jets used in inland traffic.

**Boeing 747-481D**, 1060th 747, serial number 27436, built in 1995, All Nippon Airways JA8965, delivered April 24, 1995. After having flown for a year in the "Snoopy" paint job seen on the previous page, this short-flight Jumbo used in intra-Japanese traffic (the D in the type number stands for "Domestic") bore a "Pocket Monster" paint job from mid-1998 to 2001.

**Boeing 747-481**, 979th 747, serial number 25645, built in 1993, All Nippon Airways JA 8962, delivered on June 3, 1993. From 1999 to March 2006 this plane was decorated with the "Pocket Monsters" very popular among children. On this intercontinental airplane, for reasons of identification, the airline's logo was more strongly stressed than on the sister plane shown above.

**Boeing 747-481D**, 927th 747, serial number 25642, built in 1992, All Nippon Airways JA8957, delivered on July 15, 1992. This plane, which previously was also fitted with winglets in intercontinental traffic, was painted in an especially colorful Pokemon™ pattern in May 2004.

# ANA All Nippon Airways

The All Nippon flagship Boeing 747s in particular, but not only the Jumbo-Jets, have borne special paint jobs. The fleet's smaller planes are also serving as bearers of more or less colorful advertising for the airline. Both the occasions and the paint jobs are of the most varied types. The very special jets of ANA follow no prescribed style or color code.

**Boeing 767-381**, 401st 767, serial number 25293, built in 1991, JA8357, used mainly in short flights, was delivered on November 14, 1991. In 2001 it took on an advertisement for the Japanese branch of Universal Studios.

**Boeing 767-381ER**, 883rd 767, built in 2002. JA606A was delivered to All Nippon Airlines on July 23, 2002. In July 2007 this Boeing was painted with a graphic "Panda Bear" paint job and just very small titles on its fuselage.

**Boeing 777**, 381, 160th 777, built in 1998, All Nippon Airways JA 752A. This plane, delivered on August 27, 1998, bore the simple "Winds" special paint job until 2003, a design that did not become the very long medium-flight plane very well and rather stressed than concealed its overly long proportions.

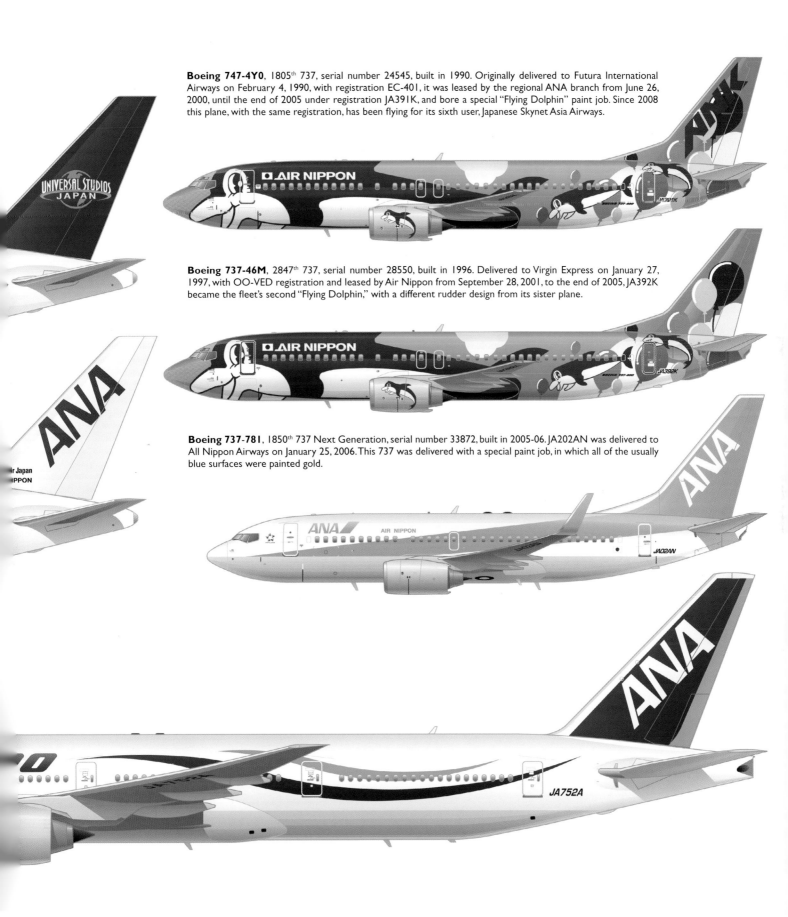

**Boeing 747-4Y0**, 1805th 737, serial number 24545, built in 1990. Originally delivered to Futura International Airways on February 4, 1990, with registration EC-401, it was leased by the regional ANA branch from June 26, 2000, until the end of 2005 under registration JA391K, and bore a special "Flying Dolphin" paint job. Since 2008 this plane, with the same registration, has been flying for its sixth user, Japanese Skynet Asia Airways.

**Boeing 737-46M**, 2847th 737, serial number 28550, built in 1996. Delivered to Virgin Express on January 27, 1997, with OO-VED registration and leased by Air Nippon from September 28, 2001, to the end of 2005, JA392K became the fleet's second "Flying Dolphin," with a different rudder design from its sister plane.

**Boeing 737-781**, 1850th 737 Next Generation, serial number 33872, built in 2005-06. JA202AN was delivered to All Nippon Airways on January 25, 2006. This 737 was delivered with a special paint job, in which all of the usually blue surfaces were painted gold.

# Avianca

Avianca, the state airline of Colombia, was founded in 1920 as one of the first airlines in South America. Today it is one of the world's oldest airlines. Since the early seventies Avianca planes have been flying in eye-catching red paint. The first specially painted planes, in 1997, were two Boeing 727s with different advertising logos. In 2000-2001 two planes were given retro paint jobs in the style of the fifties and sixties. Only a short time ago two Boeing 767s, the airline's largest planes from the early nineties to the introduction of the factory-new Airbus A330 at the end of 2008, were specially painted. A large part of the present-day fleet is leased and bears the national identification of the owners from the USA or Ireland.

**Boeing 757-2Q8**, 612th 757, serial number 26269, built in 1994. This plane, belonging to ILFC and registered N321LF, served two years with Baikal Airlines before it was leased to Avianca on August 11, 1996. There it was chosen to be painted in the line's historical style of the fifties and sixties. This paint job was used from mid-2000 until the plane was returned to ILFC in mid-2003, but the logo for the firm's 80th anniversary was applied only at the end of 2000. Since 2003 this plane has been flying for Air Finland as OH-AFJ. In 2001 a second plane, a McDonnell-Douglas MD-83 with N632CT registration, was given the retro paint job.

**Boeing 757-236**, 374th 757, serial number 25133, built in 1991. Used since June 18, 1991, by Air Europe with I-AEJA registration, it went to Avianca at the beginning of 2006 and was one of the first to bear the new paint job. In July of that year it was given Café de Colombia advertising with the well-known commercial figure Juan Valdez.

**Boeing 727-2H3**, 952nd 727, serial number 20739, built in 1973. Originally flying for Tunis Air with TS-JHO registration, it came to Avianca on a lease. Registered HK-3480X, it was given an advertising logo of the Banco Quia in 1997 shortly before the end of its career. In December 1998 the plane was mustered out and turned over to a museum.

**Boeing 767-283 ER**, 305th 767, serial number 24728, built in 1990. Its first owner was SAS, for which it served under Norwegian LN-RCC registration until 1993. In 2006 it came to Avianca and received registration N728CG. The fin bears an advertisement for Colombia.

**Boeing 767-284 ER**, 303rd 767, serial number 24742, built in 1990. This plane, originally intended for Greek Olympic Airways, was delivered to its first user, Royal Brunei Airlines, on June 8, 1990, and flew there for four years with V8-RBD registration. It has belonged to the Avianca fleet since January 1997. In 2007 the airliner was painted in an attractive new style, and was soon given equally pretty and eye-catching advertising for the national coffee industry. The painting is identical on both sides and considerably more attractive than the two other planes on these pages that bear advertising for the same sponsor. N986AN was retired in August 2009 and has been stored since.

**McDonnell-Douglas DC-9-83 (MD-83)**, 1987th DC-9, serial number 53123, built in 1992. Delivered to Avianca on May 1, 1992, the plane, flying under Irish EI-CEQ registration, was painted in new colors in 2007. At the end of 2007 the lower fuselage was given Café de Colombia advertising.

**Boeing 767-3YO ER**, 380th 767, serial number 24948, built in 1991. Delivered to Transbrasil on July 19, 1991, with PT-TAE registration, it came to Avianca in December 2004 after a period with Air Canada and was given American N948AV registration. It was painted in a simple special form for the airline's 85th anniversary. Since the end of 2006 it has flown in the considerably better-looking new Avianca standard colors introduced in the same year.

# British Airways

British Airways was born in 1974 through a merger of the long-flight airline BOAC and BEA, which flew only within Europe. By the mid-nineties it had grown into the largest international airline. British Airlines has the world's largest fleet of Boeing 747-400s in action; 56 of BA's approximately 250 planes are Jumbo-Jets, although 21 years after its introduction the first few frames have been stored. Their first special logo, "The World's Biggest Offer," appeared simultaneously on several planes in 1991.

**Boeing 747-136**, 248th 747, serial number 20953, built in 1974. G-BBPU, delivered to British Airways on March 14, 1975, was given the name "Virginia Water" in March 1990, after it had borne two different names. In 1991 the plane received "The World's Biggest Offer" labels, a large advertising action meant to revive the lowered numbers of passengers during the first Gulf War. Several other BA planes, including a 747-400, two 767-300s, and one 737-200 received similar special names. In 1999 G-BBPU was sold to a short-lived airline, Gulf Air Falcon, based in the Emirate of Sharjah, and flew a few times before being taken out of service in 2001. Another five years passed, though, until it was scrapped.

**Boeing 747-436**, 1018th 747, serial number 25811, built in 1994. G-CIVB, given the name "City of Litchfield," came to British Airways on February 15, 1994. It was given its special name at the end of 1995, with a special fin décor to recognize an international conference on the world of children.

**Boeing 747-136**, 23rd 747, serial number 19761, built in 1970. BOAC's very first 747 was delivered on April 22, 1970, but because of disagreements with the pilots' union it could only be put into service the next year. When it was mustered out on November 14, 1998, it was painted on the left side with BOAC names and the logo of the basic BA colors for a special farewell ceremony. In 1999 the Jumbo-Jet, 29 years old, was broken up in Bruntingthorpe, England.

**Boeing 737-236**, 1047<sup>th</sup> 737, serial number 23159, built in 1984. On September 14, 1994, G-BKYA was delivered to British Airways and given the name "River Derwent." The plane was delivered with an experimental paint job, with a silver (instead of white) upper fuselage. This color scheme, though, was not used throughout the fleet, for a few months later the classic blue and gray colors developed by the Landor Agency and seen on the other planes on these pages made their debut.

# British Airways

The most spectacular and PR-inspiring airline corporate identity was introduced by British Airways in mid-1997. True to the motto "The World's Favourite Airline", they began with the idea that nothing was better than making it visible. Artists all over the world were asked to develop designs in countries' typical styles and make British Airways a flying art gallery. The "Utopia" project was introduced in 1997-99 with internationally positive reactions. By that time about half the fleet had been painted thus. In Britain, though, a wave of patriotic unrest arose, headed by former Prime Minister Thatcher, who expressively threw a handkerchief over the fin of a model.

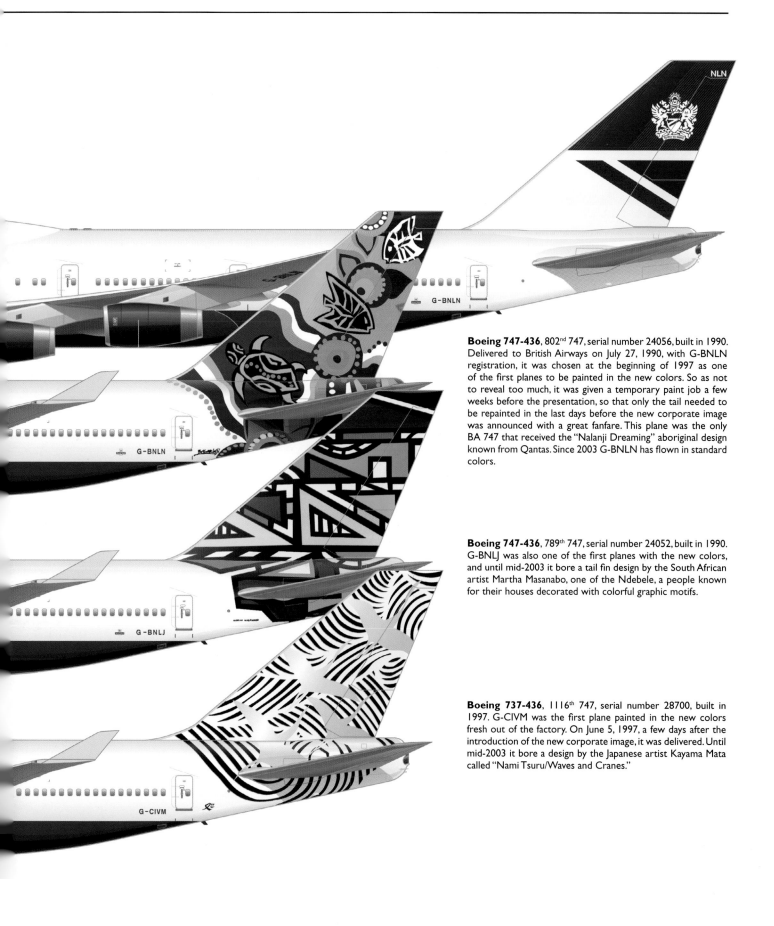

**Boeing 747-436**, 802ⁿᵈ 747, serial number 24056, built in 1990. Delivered to British Airways on July 27, 1990, with G-BNLN registration, it was chosen at the beginning of 1997 as one of the first planes to be painted in the new colors. So as not to reveal too much, it was given a temporary paint job a few weeks before the presentation, so that only the tail needed to be repainted in the last days before the new corporate image was announced with a great fanfare. This plane was the only BA 747 that received the "Nalanji Dreaming" aboriginal design known from Qantas. Since 2003 G-BNLN has flown in standard colors.

**Boeing 747-436**, 789ᵗʰ 747, serial number 24052, built in 1990. G-BNLJ was also one of the first planes with the new colors, and until mid-2003 it bore a tail fin design by the South African artist Martha Masanabo, one of the Ndebele, a people known for their houses decorated with colorful graphic motifs.

**Boeing 737-436**, 1116ᵗʰ 747, serial number 28700, built in 1997. G-CIVM was the first plane painted in the new colors fresh out of the factory. On June 5, 1997, a few days after the introduction of the new corporate image, it was delivered. Until mid-2003 it bore a design by the Japanese artist Kayama Mata called "Nami Tsuru/Waves and Cranes."

# British Airways

The new corporate identity of 1997 was a fantastic idea, but perhaps the responsible parties of "The World's Favorite Airline" were simply gone on the premise that their firm still was called BRITISH Airways. Delft tiles or Chinese calligraphy on a British plane were simply too foreign, to many British people, to represent their country. Then, too, the fact that British motifs developed at that time were used too rarely in the beginning. When the lovely British designs like "Chelsea Rose" finally appeared it was already too late to change public opinion.

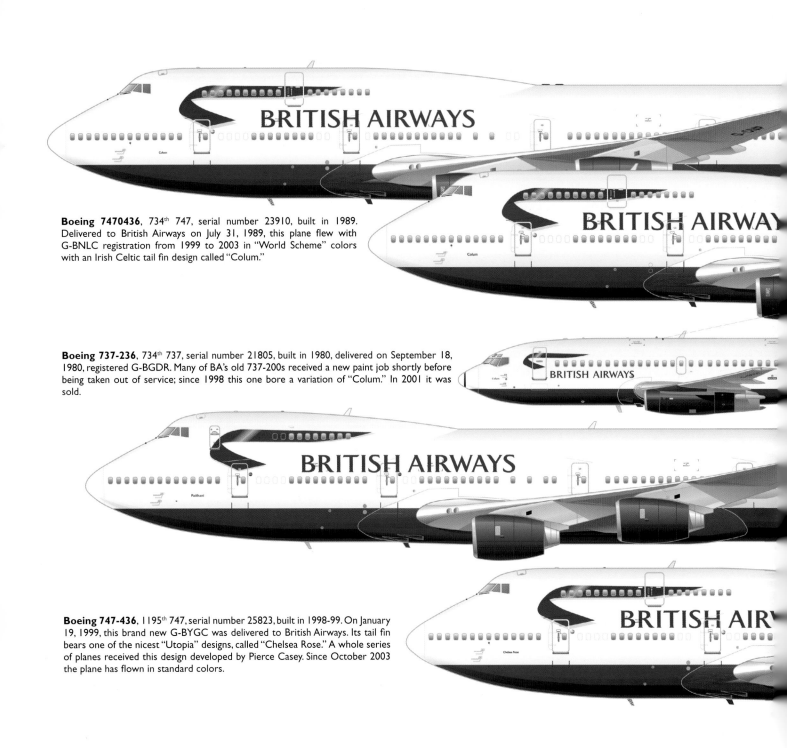

**Boeing 7470436**, 734th 747, serial number 23910, built in 1989. Delivered to British Airways on July 31, 1989, this plane flew with G-BNLC registration from 1999 to 2003 in "World Scheme" colors with an Irish Celtic tail fin design called "Colum."

**Boeing 737-236**, 734th 737, serial number 21805, built in 1980, delivered on September 18, 1980, registered G-BGDR. Many of BA's old 737-200s received a new paint job shortly before being taken out of service; since 1998 this one bore a variation of "Colum." In 2001 it was sold.

**Boeing 747-436**, 1195th 747, serial number 25823, built in 1998-99. On January 19, 1999, this brand new G-BYGC was delivered to British Airways. Its tail fin bears one of the nicest "Utopia" designs, called "Chelsea Rose." A whole series of planes received this design developed by Pierce Casey. Since October 2003 the plane has flown in standard colors.

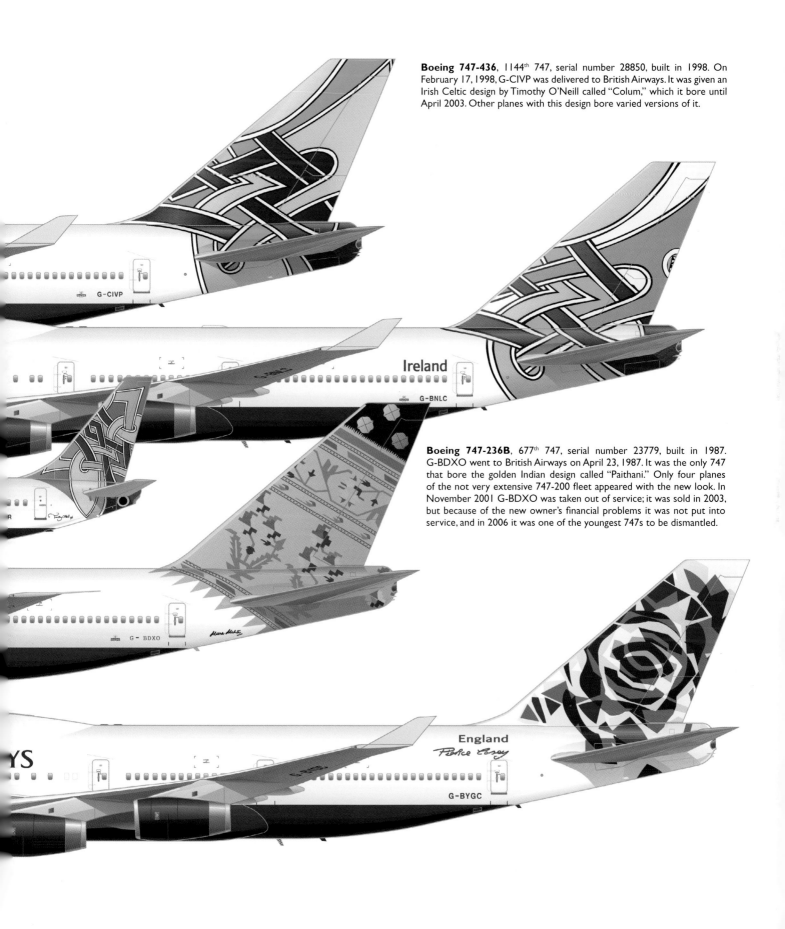

**Boeing 747-436**, 1144th 747, serial number 28850, built in 1998. On February 17, 1998, G-CIVP was delivered to British Airways. It was given an Irish Celtic design by Timothy O'Neill called "Colum," which it bore until April 2003. Other planes with this design bore varied versions of it.

**Boeing 747-236B**, 677th 747, serial number 23779, built in 1987. G-BDXO went to British Airways on April 23, 1987. It was the only 747 that bore the golden Indian design called "Paithani." Only four planes of the not very extensive 747-200 fleet appeared with the new look. In November 2001 G-BDXO was taken out of service; it was sold in 2003, but because of the new owner's financial problems it was not put into service, and in 2006 it was one of the youngest 747s to be dismantled.

# British Airways

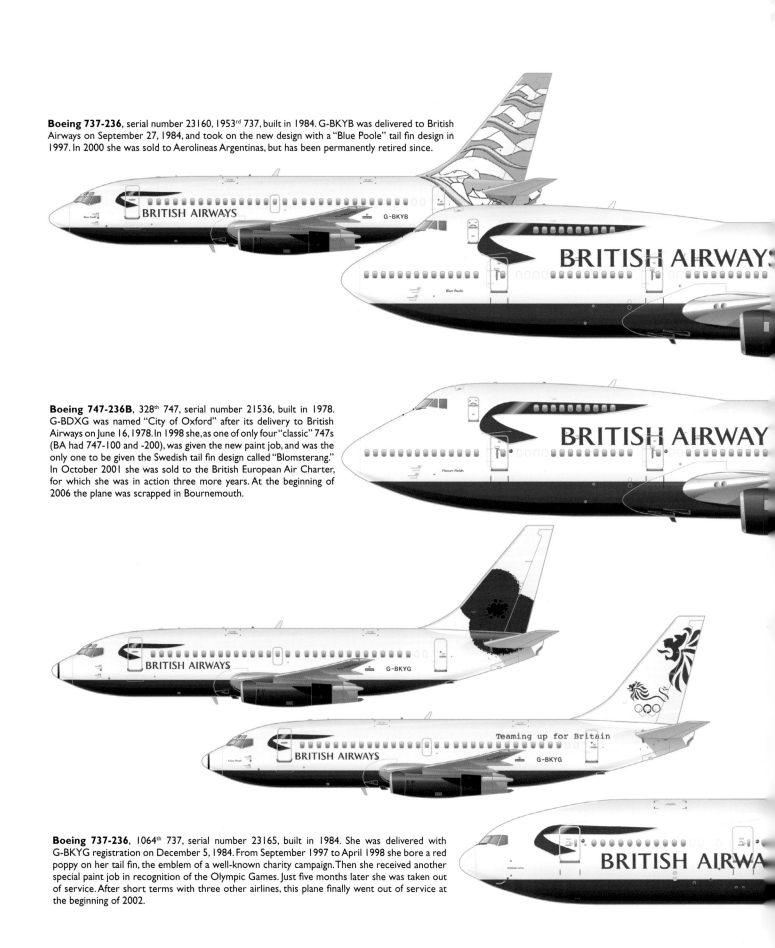

**Boeing 737-236**, serial number 23160, 1953rd 737, built in 1984. G-BKYB was delivered to British Airways on September 27, 1984, and took on the new design with a "Blue Poole" tail fin design in 1997. In 2000 she was sold to Aerolineas Argentinas, but has been permanently retired since.

**Boeing 747-236B**, 328th 747, serial number 21536, built in 1978. G-BDXG was named "City of Oxford" after its delivery to British Airways on June 16, 1978. In 1998 she, as one of only four "classic" 747s (BA had 747-100 and -200), was given the new paint job, and was the only one to be given the Swedish tail fin design called "Blomsterang." In October 2001 she was sold to the British European Air Charter, for which she was in action three more years. At the beginning of 2006 the plane was scrapped in Bournemouth.

**Boeing 737-236**, 1064th 737, serial number 23165, built in 1984. She was delivered with G-BKYG registration on December 5, 1984. From September 1997 to April 1998 she bore a red poppy on her tail fin, the emblem of a well-known charity campaign. Then she received another special paint job in recognition of the Olympic Games. Just five months later she was taken out of service. After short terms with three other airlines, this plane finally went out of service at the beginning of 2002.

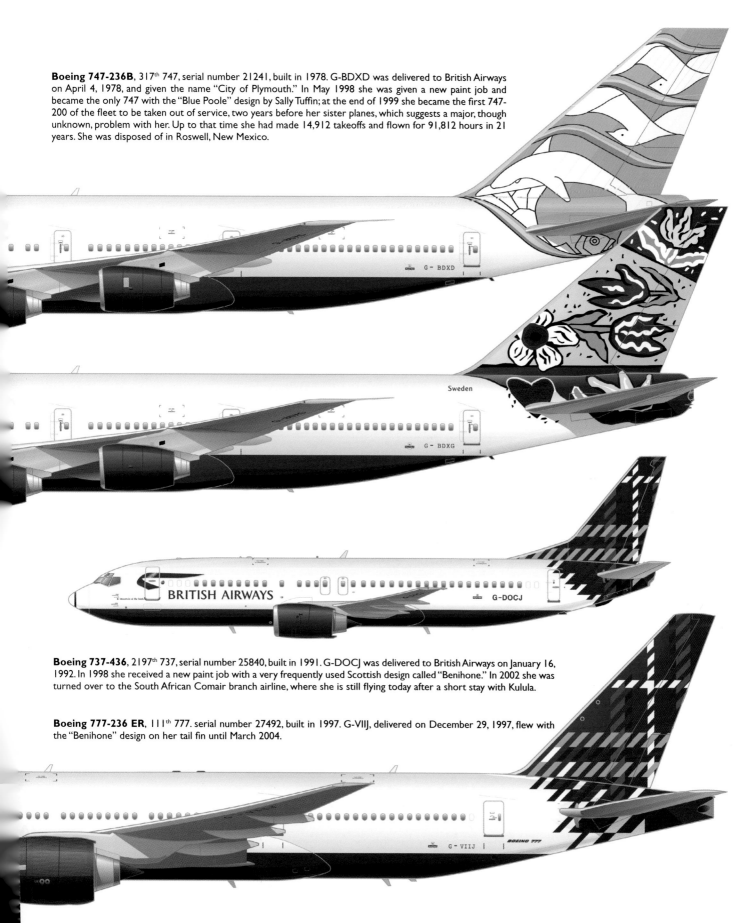

**Boeing 747-236B**, 317th 747, serial number 21241, built in 1978. G-BDXD was delivered to British Airways on April 4, 1978, and given the name "City of Plymouth." In May 1998 she was given a new paint job and became the only 747 with the "Blue Poole" design by Sally Tuffin; at the end of 1999 she became the first 747-200 of the fleet to be taken out of service, two years before her sister planes, which suggests a major, though unknown, problem with her. Up to that time she had made 14,912 takeoffs and flown for 91,812 hours in 21 years. She was disposed of in Roswell, New Mexico.

**Boeing 737-436**, 2197th 737, serial number 25840, built in 1991. G-DOCJ was delivered to British Airways on January 16, 1992. In 1998 she received a new paint job with a very frequently used Scottish design called "Benihone." In 2002 she was turned over to the South African Comair branch airline, where she is still flying today after a short stay with Kulula.

**Boeing 777-236 ER**, 111th 777. serial number 27492, built in 1997. G-VIIJ, delivered on December 29, 1997, flew with the "Benihone" design on her tail fin until March 2004.

# British Airways

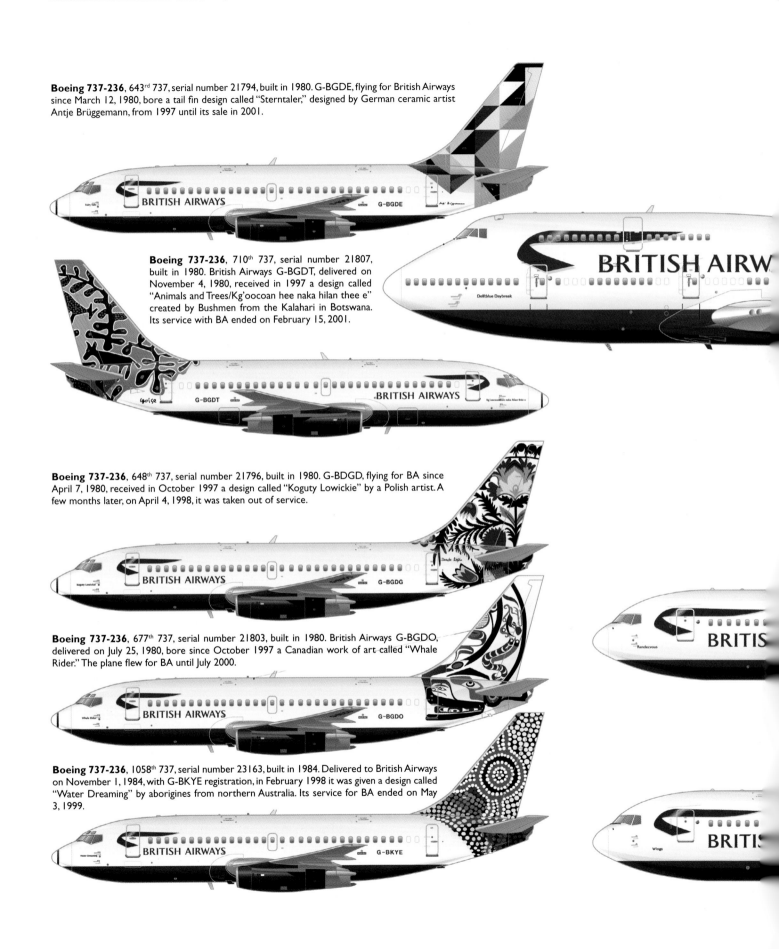

**Boeing 737-236**, 643rd 737, serial number 21794, built in 1980. G-BGDE, flying for British Airways since March 12, 1980, bore a tail fin design called "Sterntaler," designed by German ceramic artist Antje Brüggemann, from 1997 until its sale in 2001.

**Boeing 737-236**, 710th 737, serial number 21807, built in 1980. British Airways G-BGDT, delivered on November 4, 1980, received in 1997 a design called "Animals and Trees/Kg'oocoan hee naka hilan thee e" created by Bushmen from the Kalahari in Botswana. Its service with BA ended on February 15, 2001.

**Boeing 737-236**, 648th 737, serial number 21796, built in 1980. G-BDGD, flying for BA since April 7, 1980, received in October 1997 a design called "Koguty Lowickie" by a Polish artist. A few months later, on April 4, 1998, it was taken out of service.

**Boeing 737-236**, 677th 737, serial number 21803, built in 1980. British Airways G-BGDO, delivered on July 25, 1980, bore since October 1997 a Canadian work of art called "Whale Rider." The plane flew for BA until July 2000.

**Boeing 737-236**, 1058th 737, serial number 23163, built in 1984. Delivered to British Airways on November 1, 1984, with G-BKYE registration, in February 1998 it was given a design called "Water Dreaming" by aborigines from northern Australia. Its service for BA ended on May 3, 1999.

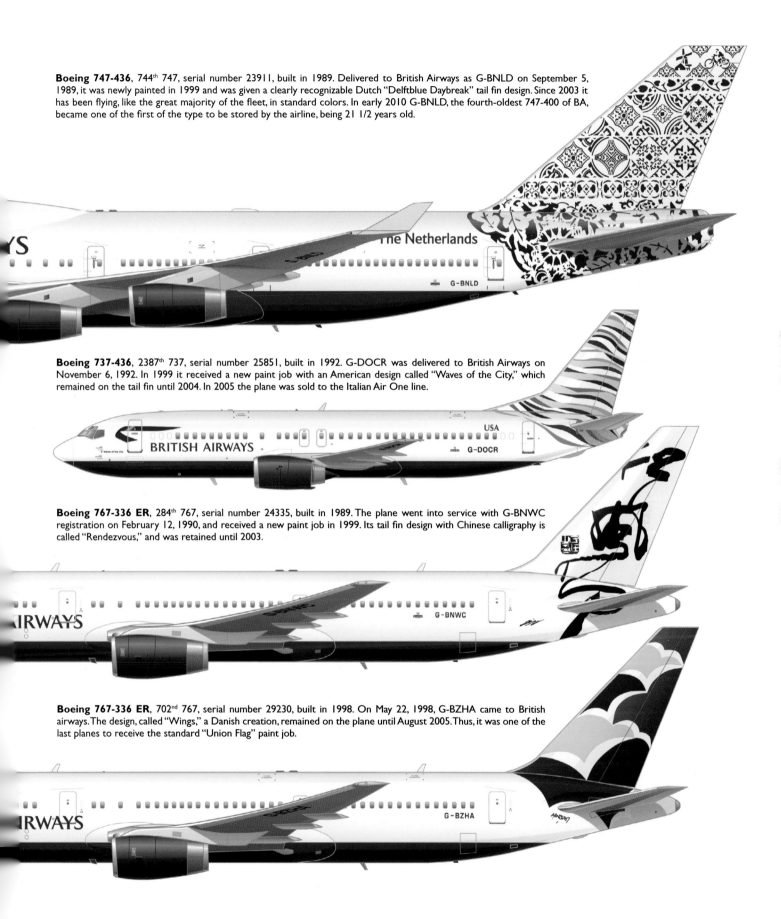

**Boeing 747-436**, 744th 747, serial number 23911, built in 1989. Delivered to British Airways as G-BNLD on September 5, 1989, it was newly painted in 1999 and was given a clearly recognizable Dutch "Delftblue Daybreak" tail fin design. Since 2003 it has been flying, like the great majority of the fleet, in standard colors. In early 2010 G-BNLD, the fourth-oldest 747-400 of BA, became one of the first of the type to be stored by the airline, being 21 1/2 years old.

The Netherlands

G-BNLD

**Boeing 737-436**, 2387th 737, serial number 25851, built in 1992. G-DOCR was delivered to British Airways on November 6, 1992. In 1999 it received a new paint job with an American design called "Waves of the City," which remained on the tail fin until 2004. In 2005 the plane was sold to the Italian Air One line.

BRITISH AIRWAYS

USA

G-DOCR

**Boeing 767-336 ER**, 284th 767, serial number 24335, built in 1989. The plane went into service with G-BNWC registration on February 12, 1990, and received a new paint job in 1999. Its tail fin design with Chinese calligraphy is called "Rendezvous," and was retained until 2003.

AIRWAYS

G-BNWC

**Boeing 767-336 ER**, 702nd 767, serial number 29230, built in 1998. On May 22, 1998, G-BZHA came to British airways. The design, called "Wings," a Danish creation, remained on the plane until August 2005. Thus, it was one of the last planes to receive the standard "Union Flag" paint job.

AIRWAYS

G-BZHA

# British Airways

In 2001 one of the British motifs, called "Chatham Historic Dockyard," which had actually been designed only for the Concorde, was finally declared to be the standard livery. By 2005 all the "world tails" had thus been painted over. Since then a few specially painted or labeled planes have promoted special events on this basis.

**Boeing 747-436**, 789th 747, serial number 24052, built in 1990. This plane was delivered on May 23, 1990. Since 1986, British Airways has put on a free flight once a year for underprivileged children. On this occasion the plane in question, a different Boeing 747 every year, is supplied with "Dreamflight" titles. For the 20th anniversary G-BNLJ bore the appropriate additional markings from October 2006 to March 2007.

**Boeing 747-436**, 1144th 747, serial number 28850, built in 1998. Since February 17, 1998, G-CIVP has flown for British Airways. Until it received the standard BA livery in April 2003, its tail fin had been decorated with the Celtic "Colum" design for five years (see pp. 46-47). In February 2005 it bore "Backing the Bid" labels on the occasion of London's eventually successful campaign for the 2012 Olympic Games. At the end of January 2009 it became a logo jet when adhesive "Oneworld" airline alliance labels were applied.

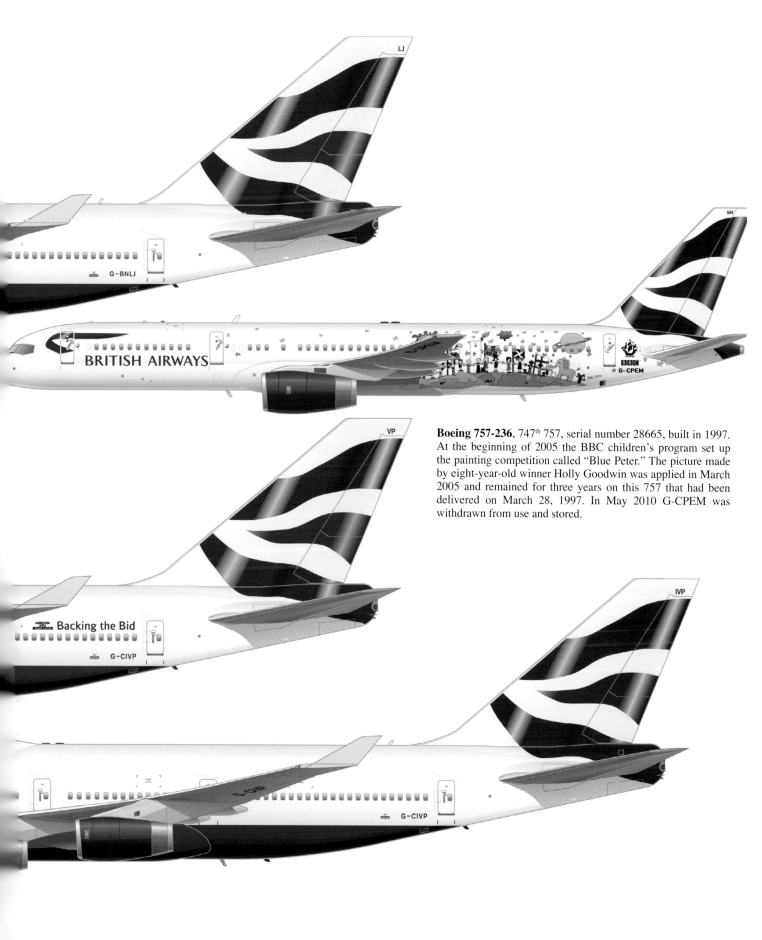

**Boeing 757-236**, 747<sup>th</sup> 757, serial number 28665, built in 1997. At the beginning of 2005 the BBC children's program set up the painting competition called "Blue Peter." The picture made by eight-year-old winner Holly Goodwin was applied in March 2005 and remained for three years on this 757 that had been delivered on March 28, 1997. In May 2010 G-CPEM was withdrawn from use and stored.

# Cathay Pacific Airways

Hong Kong's renowned Cathay Pacific Airways, staying in the top rank of favorite international airlines for years, has also experienced the advertising reality of striking special paint jobs, but rather late to be sure, only in 1997. But the rare "colorful birds" of CX, four of them to date, are all very tastefully and impressively painted, and justly so in view of the airline's corporate image.

**Airbus A330-343X**, 776th A330/340, built in 2006. Put into service on August 30, 2006, B-LAD bears a special livery that it displays as 100th member of the air fleet. It was also labeled for the airline's 60th anniversary; the latter stickers were removed two years later.

**Boeing 747-467F**, 1255th 747, serial number 30804, built in 2000. B-HUL came to Cathay Pacific on September 12, 2000. In 2006 the airline decided to remove the fuselage colors of all their freighters, as this promised a small savings in fuel because of the lighter weight. A large number of the 747 freighter fleet thus had their paint removed, B-HUL in July 2006, until it was found that this means accomplished practically nothing. Since then newly arriving 747 freighters have borne the standard livery, although the metallically shimmering planes certainly looked spectacular.

**Boeing 747-267B**, 466th 747, serial number 25351, built in 1980. Put into service in 1980 with VR-HIB registration, in 1997 it became the first Cathay Pacific plane with special painting, a very attractive design showing the skyline of the economic center. Named "Spirit of Hong Kong" in honor of the return of the British Crown colony of Hong Kong to China in 1997, it was registered B-HIB at almost the same time. At the end of 1997 the 747 was leased to Air Atlanta and registered TF-ATC. It was taken out of service in 2004 and scrapped a little later. A very similar livery was used from the beginning of 2000 to 2003 on the Boeing 747-467 registered B-HOX.

# Cathay Pacific Airways

**Boeing 747-467**, 887th 747, serial number 25351, built in 1991. Cathay Pacific put this plane, registered VR-HOY, into service on December 22, 1991. After Hong Kong was returned to China in 1997 it was given B-HOY registration. In the summer of 2002 it received an attractive paint job meant to advertise Hong Kong's special role as an economic center. It flew in these colors for six years before receiving the standard livery in 2008. Note: For reasons of space the top and front views of B-HOY are in a smaller scale.

**Boeing 777-367 ER**, 692nd 777, serial number 36832, built in 2008. B-KPF, delivered on January 30, 2008, was given the attractive "Asia's world city" livery that was previously used on the 747-467 shown above. Because the "Triple Seven" is proportioned a bit too long the design is not quite as charming as it was on the 747, which remains the more attractive "billboard."

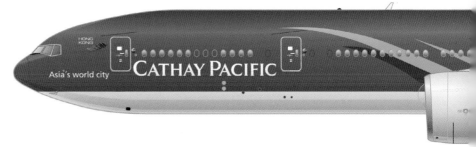

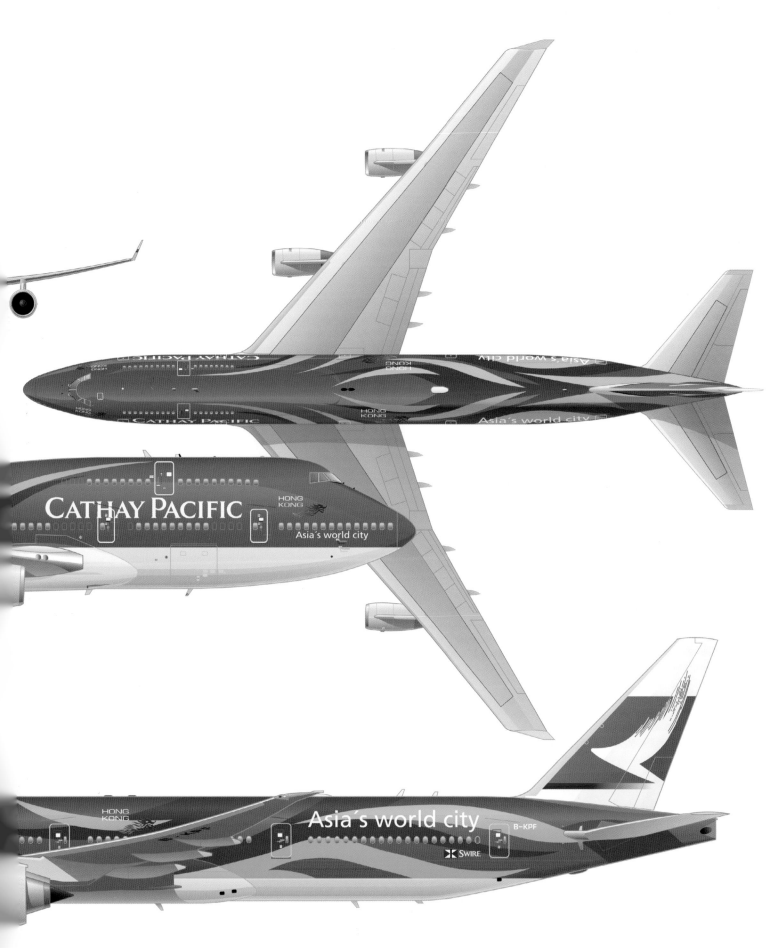

CATHAY PACIFIC

HONG KONG

Asia's world city

Asia's world city

B-KPF

SWIRE

# China Airlines

Taiwan's national airline, with its striking paint jobs, is nevertheless not a protagonist of special liveries. Since 2005, though, a few "colorful birds" have been integrated into the fleet. Along with the world-renowned 747-400 in Boeing Dreamliner livery there are two A330-300s and one 737-800. The fleet of China Airlines, some 70 airplanes, is composed, interestingly, mainly of long-flight planes and freighters; the short-flight fleet, on the other hand, is unusually small.

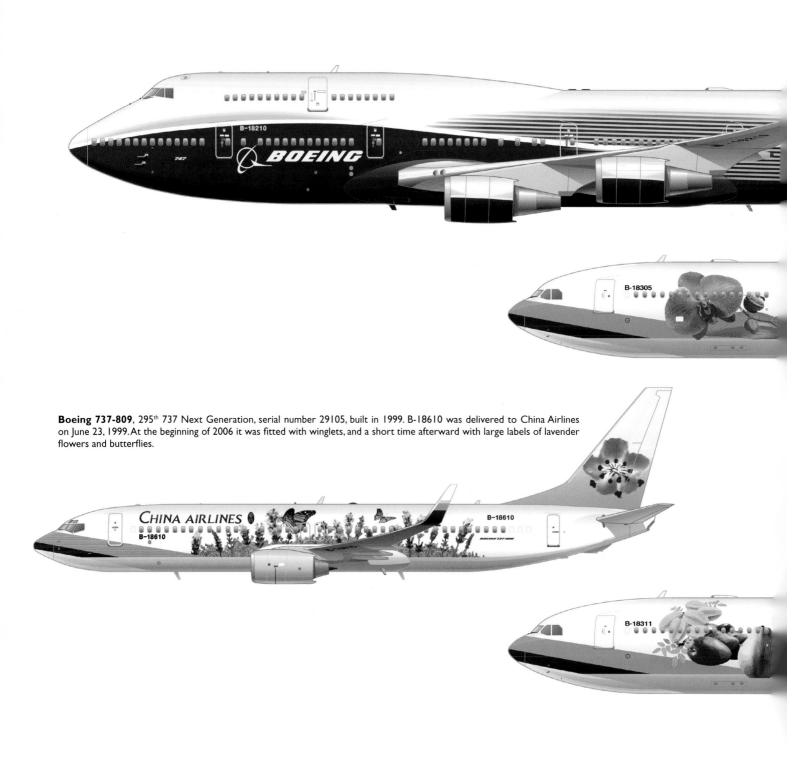

**Boeing 737-809**, 295th 737 Next Generation, serial number 29105, built in 1999. B-18610 was delivered to China Airlines on June 23, 1999. At the beginning of 2006 it was fitted with winglets, and a short time afterward with large labels of lavender flowers and butterflies.

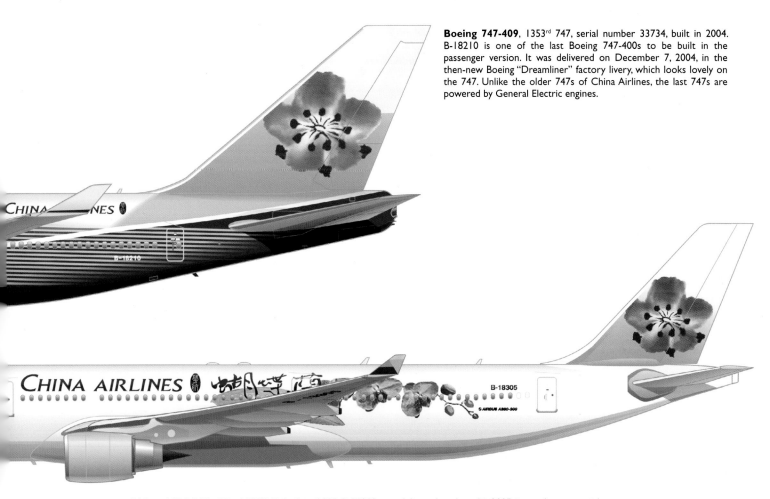

**Boeing 747-409**, 1353rd 747, serial number 33734, built in 2004. B-18210 is one of the last Boeing 747-400s to be built in the passenger version. It was delivered on December 7, 2004, in the then-new Boeing "Dreamliner" factory livery, which looks lovely on the 747. Unlike the older 747s of China Airlines, the last 747s are powered by General Electric engines.

**Airbus A330-302**, 671st A330/340, built in 2005. B-18305 was delivered on June 16, 2005, in an elegant special livery called "Butterfly Orchid" and decorated with orchids.

**Airbus A330-302**, 752nd A330/340, built in 2006. This plane bore the "Fruit Sweet" design since being delivered on June 21, 2006. It is not a paint job, but is made of large adhesive labels.

# Chinesische Airlines

The number of airlines in the People's Republic of China has really exploded since 1990. Yet it took a long time until, among the hundreds of commercial airplanes in mainland China, the first special paint job was seen. Since then, though, many airlines have made active use of this marketing idea. A selection can be seen here.

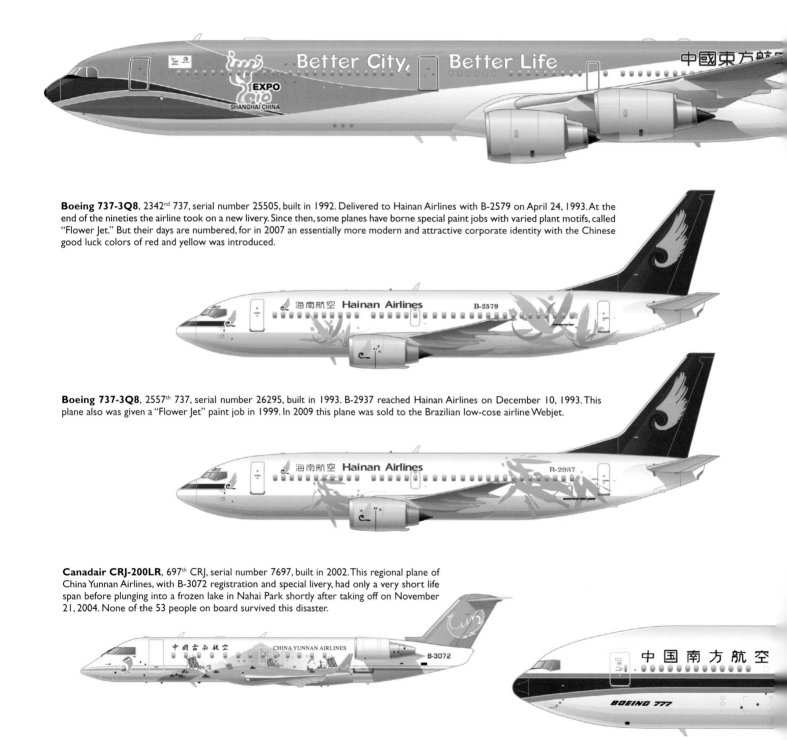

**Boeing 737-3Q8**, 2342nd 737, serial number 25505, built in 1992. Delivered to Hainan Airlines with B-2579 on April 24, 1993. At the end of the nineties the airline took on a new livery. Since then, some planes have borne special paint jobs with varied plant motifs, called "Flower Jet." But their days are numbered, for in 2007 an essentially more modern and attractive corporate identity with the Chinese good luck colors of red and yellow was introduced.

**Boeing 737-3Q8**, 2557th 737, serial number 26295, built in 1993. B-2937 reached Hainan Airlines on December 10, 1993. This plane also was given a "Flower Jet" paint job in 1999. In 2009 this plane was sold to the Brazilian low-cose airline Webjet.

**Canadair CRJ-200LR**, 697th CRJ, serial number 7697, built in 2002. This regional plane of China Yunnan Airlines, with B-3072 registration and special livery, had only a very short life span before plunging into a frozen lake in Nahai Park shortly after taking off on November 21, 2004. None of the 53 people on board survived this disaster.

**Airbus A340-642**, 586<sup>th</sup> A330/340, built in 2004. China Eastern received B-6055 on August 15, 2004. On the occasion of the Expo 2010 in Shanghai the airline had this plane given its special paint job in March 2006.

CHINA EASTERN  B-6055

© AIRBUS A340-600

**Boeing 737-330 (F)**, 1514<sup>th</sup> 737, serial number 23837, built in 1988. This plane, first in service with Condor with D-ABWE registration, was rebuilt as a freighter during its time with Lufthansa. Since February 2003 it has been leased by Yangtze River Express. B-5057 received this airy special paint job which she bore until 2007, before being given the airline's new red and yellow livery.

Yangtze River Express  B-5057

**Airbus A321-231**, 908<sup>th</sup> A319/320/321, built in 1998. This plane, delivered to Air Macau on February 4, 1999, with CS-MAJ registration, was re-registered as B-MAJ in 2000, and at the beginning of 2002 it was given large labels with the logo of the Asian soccer championship, held in Macau in 2005. At the end of 2005 it was finally given a striking new special paint job to honor this important sporting event, and is still to be seen in it more than four years after the event.

AIR MACAU  澳門航空  *Macau* 2005  4th East Asian Games  B-MAJ

**Boeing 777-21B**, 20<sup>th</sup> 777, serial number 27357, built in 1996. China Southern was one of the first airlines to put a Triple Seven into service. B-2051 was their first plane of this type, and was delivered on February 28, 1996. In 2006-07 it bore advertising logos for the introduction of the Toyota Camry scattered seemingly at random over the fuselage. In 2008 the airline announced that its 777s were up for sale, but as we went to press no buyers had been found.

TOYOTA  广汽 TOYOTA  CAMRY  B-2051  CHINA SOUTHERN  凯美瑞  TOYOTA

# Condor

Condor contracted in 1999 with the well-known American artist James Rizzi to create a design for a Boeing 757-200 for the firm's 40th anniversary. This colorful "Rizzi-Bird" flew until 2004. The second Condor plane with a special paint job is one of the fleet's thirteen 757-300s. Condor is one of the few users of this type of plane, which is certainly economical but commercially unsuccessful, and was produced for only five years, from 1999 to 2004.

**Boeing 757-330**, 929th 757, serial number 29023, built in 2000. D-ABON was delivered to Condor on June 2, 2000, and though renamed Thomas Cook for a time, retained its original yellow paint until the beginning of 2006, when it received this hearty new paint job for Condor's 50th anniversary with the slogan of the advertising campaign of the time. The plane was also given the name "Willi."

**Boeing 767-232**, twelfth 767, serial number 22214, built in 1982. The "Spirit of Delta" was a special plane for that airline. Until it was taken out of service it always bore special names or liveries. Here it is shown in its most unusual colors, which it received in 2004 on the occasion of the firm's 75th anniversary, a retro painting that actually was not a precise reproduction of a historical livery. A good year later it was given the old livery of the eighties in preparation for being taken out of service. Since 2006 it has been a museum piece.

**Boeing 737-232**, 1006th 737, serial number 23082, built in 1984. N310DA joined the Delta Air Lines fleet on February 8, 1984. From July 2000 to August 2002 it flew in a "Powerpuff Girls" logo for the Cartoon Network. Since the end of 2006 the plane has been flying under OD-LMB registration for the Lebanon Flying Carpet.

Delta Air Lines, one of the world's most important airlines, merged with Northwest Airlines in 2009. The world's numerically largest fleet, formerly a very boring twin-jet monoculture, is now centered in Atlanta, Georgia, and has become much more interesting thanks to the "inherited" planes from its northern ex-rival. Delta has used special paint jobs again and again, the most eye-catching being those of 1996 for the Olympic Games in its home town.

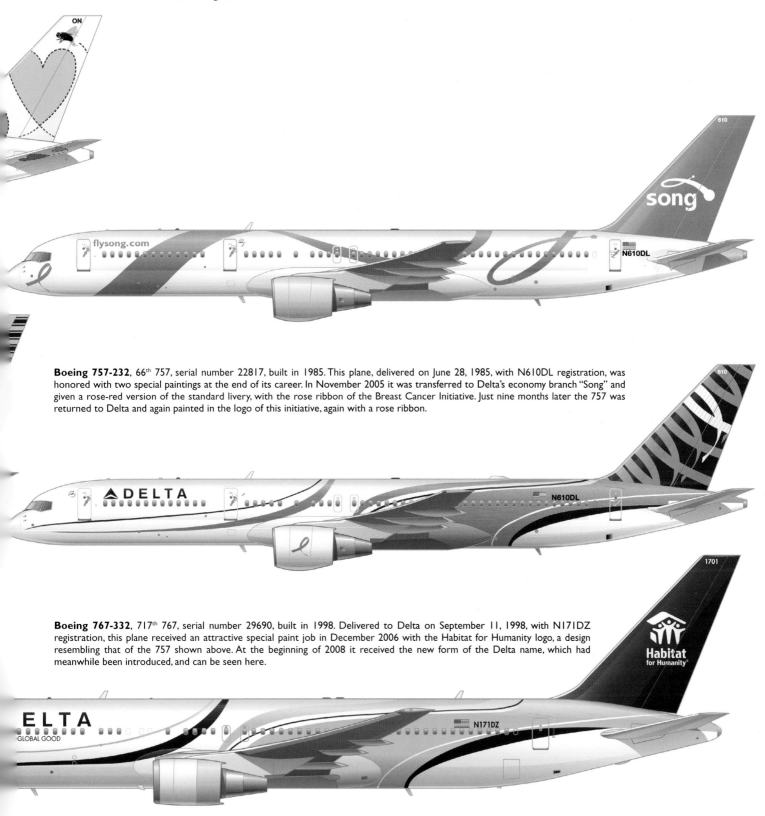

**Boeing 757-232**, 66th 757, serial number 22817, built in 1985. This plane, delivered on June 28, 1985, with N610DL registration, was honored with two special paintings at the end of its career. In November 2005 it was transferred to Delta's economy branch "Song" and given a rose-red version of the standard livery, with the rose ribbon of the Breast Cancer Initiative. Just nine months later the 757 was returned to Delta and again painted in the logo of this initiative, again with a rose ribbon.

**Boeing 767-332**, 717th 767, serial number 29690, built in 1998. Delivered to Delta on September 11, 1998, with N171DZ registration, this plane received an attractive special paint job in December 2006 with the Habitat for Humanity logo, a design resembling that of the 757 shown above. At the beginning of 2008 it received the new form of the Delta name, which had meanwhile been introduced, and can be seen here.

# Emirates, Etihad, Gulf Air

The United Arab Emirates have developed three important international airlines: Gulf Air, located in Bahrain; Emirates from Dubai; and Etihad from Abu Dhabi. Gulf Air is richest in tradition, Emirates by far the biggest, but the young Etihad is also growing quickly. While Gulf Air and Etihad have already used several airplanes with special liveries, Emirates has surprisingly refrained from doing so to date, even though many planes of their fleet have been used seasonally for advertising purposes.

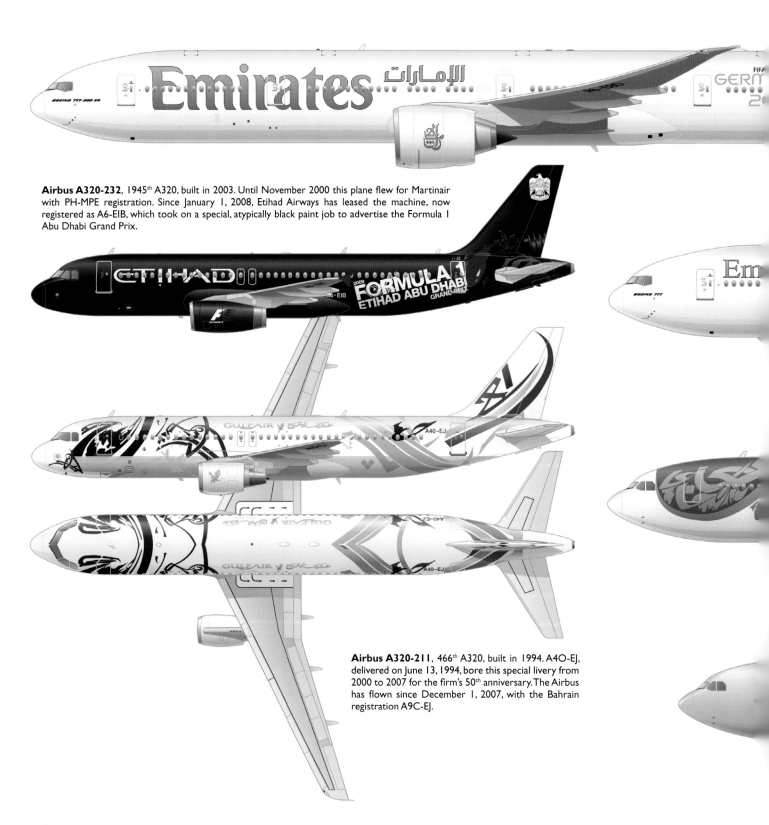

**Airbus A320-232**, 1945th A320, built in 2003. Until November 2000 this plane flew for Martinair with PH-MPE registration. Since January 1, 2008, Etihad Airways has leased the machine, now registered as A6-EIB, which took on a special, atypically black paint job to advertise the Formula 1 Abu Dhabi Grand Prix.

**Airbus A320-211**, 466th A320, built in 1994. A4O-EJ, delivered on June 13, 1994, bore this special livery from 2000 to 2007 for the firm's 50th anniversary. The Airbus has flown since December 1, 2007, with the Bahrain registration A9C-EJ.

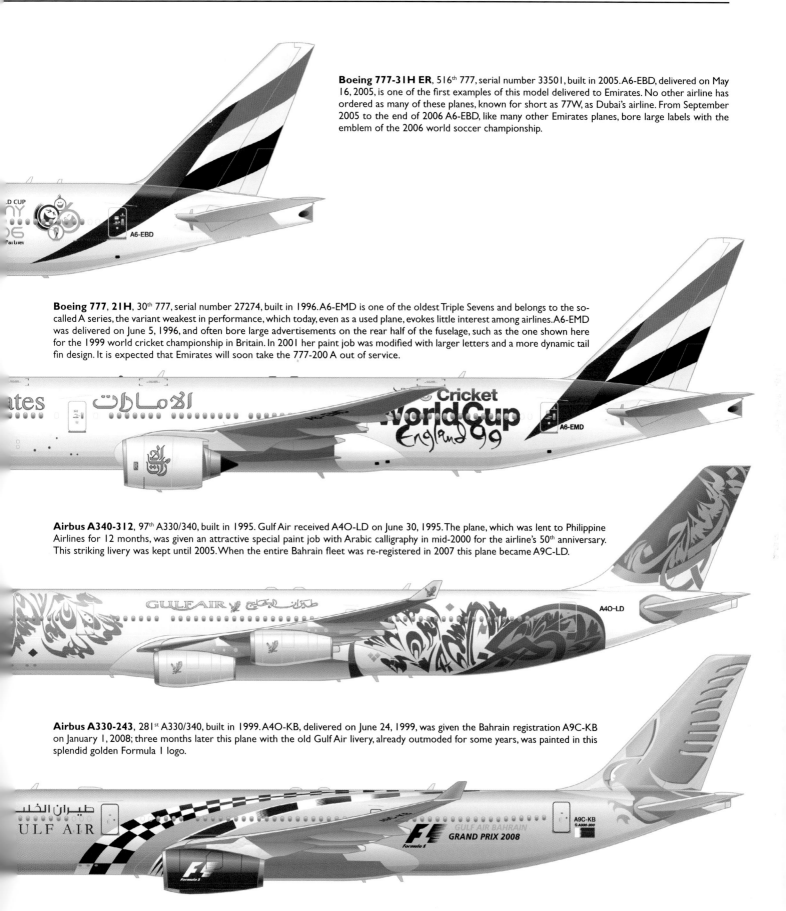

**Boeing 777-31H ER**, 516th 777, serial number 33501, built in 2005. A6-EBD, delivered on May 16, 2005, is one of the first examples of this model delivered to Emirates. No other airline has ordered as many of these planes, known for short as 77W, as Dubai's airline. From September 2005 to the end of 2006 A6-EBD, like many other Emirates planes, bore large labels with the emblem of the 2006 world soccer championship.

A6-EBD

**Boeing 777, 21H**, 30th 777, serial number 27274, built in 1996. A6-EMD is one of the oldest Triple Sevens and belongs to the so-called A series, the variant weakest in performance, which today, even as a used plane, evokes little interest among airlines. A6-EMD was delivered on June 5, 1996, and often bore large advertisements on the rear half of the fuselage, such as the one shown here for the 1999 world cricket championship in Britain. In 2001 her paint job was modified with larger letters and a more dynamic tail fin design. It is expected that Emirates will soon take the 777-200 A out of service.

Cricket World Cup England 99    A6-EMD

**Airbus A340-312**, 97th A330/340, built in 1995. Gulf Air received A4O-LD on June 30, 1995. The plane, which was lent to Philippine Airlines for 12 months, was given an attractive special paint job with Arabic calligraphy in mid-2000 for the airline's 50th anniversary. This striking livery was kept until 2005. When the entire Bahrain fleet was re-registered in 2007 this plane became A9C-LD.

GULF AIR    A4O-LD

**Airbus A330-243**, 281st A330/340, built in 1999. A4O-KB, delivered on June 24, 1999, was given the Bahrain registration A9C-KB on January 1, 2008; three months later this plane with the old Gulf Air livery, already outmoded for some years, was painted in this splendid golden Formula 1 logo.

ULF AIR    GULF AIR BAHRAIN    GRAND PRIX 2008    A9C-KB

# Eva Air

Eva Air, founded in 1989 and belonging to the Evergreen Group, and now Taiwan's second largest airline, introduced a striking new livery in 2002; in the ensuing years it became the basis for several special versions.

**Airbus A330-203**, 555ᵗʰ A330/340, built in 2003. B-16303 was delivered to Eva Air on February 4, 2004, and flew for a year as a completely normal member of the fleet before receiving a special "Hello Kitty" paint job in 2005. The sister plane, B-16309, was given a very similar decoration a year later.

**Boeing 777-35E ER**, 524ᵗʰ 777, serial number 32639, built in 2005. B-16701, delivered on June 14, 2005, is Eva Air's first Triple Seven. The Taiwanese carrier will replace its Boeing 747-400s, which are currently in the process of being converted as freighters, with this model in the course of time. The first three 777s were given the special livery shown here, with which the airline sought to call attention to itself as one of the first users of the 777-300R, which became more and more of a bestseller of the series recently. Note: for reasons of space the top view is shown in a smaller scale.

# Finnair

"The Official Airline of Santa Claus" is what the Finnish flag carrier Finnair calls itself every Christmas. And every year one or more planes are chosen to take Santa for a ride. In 2010 Finnair became the last regular passenger airline which retired the MD-11, last of the three-jet planes, in passenger service. Since 2006 its long-range fleet has been completed with A340-300s. For this version of the A340 Finnair is a special customer, the last airline to order these long successful, elegant airliners.

**McDonnell Douglas MD-11**, 479th DC-10/MD-11, serial number 48450, built in 1991. OH-LGB, delivered to Finnair on July 12, 1991, was given its present livery in 2001. Since the end of 2005 it has borne the "Official Airline of Santa Claus" labels in the winter, with Santa shown on the middle of the fuselage, and in the summers of 2006 to 2008 the "Moomins" labels of a popular Finnish comic strip, shown here. In addition, for unknown reasons, the gray lower fuselages of almost all Finnair planes were painted white in 2007. OH-LGB was stored at the beginning of 2010.

**Airbus A340-311**, 58th A330/340, built in 1994. After barely twelve years in service with Virgin Atlantic this plane, formerly registered as G-VFLY, was sold to Finnair in the spring of 2006. As the fleet's first A340 it was registered OH-LQA. Shortly after being put into service by Finnair it was made into a Christmas plane with the appropriate decorations.

**Airbus A340-313X**, 844th A330/340, built in 2007. OH-LQC was delivered to Finnair on June 21, 2007. The plane is thus one of the last A340s of the 300 series to be built. At Christmas in 2007 it received Santa Claus labels, which were replaced for the summer of 2008 by the same "Moomins" type as were already used on the MD-11 shown above.

*Official airline of Santa Claus*

OH-LGB

BOEING MD-11

**Airbus A319-112**, 1808th A319/320/321, built in 2002. OH-LVF was painted in the "One World" airline alliance logo in the summer of 2008, along with the factory-new Airbus A340 OH-LQE.

FINNAIR
oneworld

OH-LVF

**Airbus A319-112**, 1791st A319/320/321, built in 2002. Delivered to Finnair with OH-LVE registration, this plane was chosen to bear a retro livery in 1950s style as of July 2008; it looks great on the A319. At the same time it was named "Silver Bird."

FINNISH AIRLINES

finnair

OH-LVE

Silver Bird

# Germanwings

It terms of special paint jobs German airlines are latecomers. Only since the end of the 1990s has the style emerged, but since then several colorful birds have been seen over the Federal Republic. Germanwings had or has a number of planes in many colors in service, most of them as flying billboards.

**Airbus A319-112**, 1277th A319/320/321, built in 2000, delivered to US Airways on July 21, 2000, as N743UW. Since going to Germanwings in 2005 it has borne "Spirit of T-Mobile" advertising. Its sister plane D-AKNR also flew with Deutsche Telekom advertising, but for the "T-Com," its upper fuselage in white and tail fin in magenta. Both of these planes were repainted in standard livery in early 2009.

**Airbus A319-114**, 700th A319/320/321, built in 1997, delivered to Lufthansa on September 12, 1997. Leased by Germanwings from 2004 to 2007, it was given the logo of the Cologne-Bonn Airport.

**Airbus A319-112**, 1089th A319/320/321, built in 1999. The former N720UW was delivered to US Airways on September 29, 1999. Since going to Germanwings in 2005, it bears Baden-Württemberg advertising on the basis of the standard livery.

**Airbus A319-112**, 1147th A319/320/321, built in 1999, delivered to US Airways as N727UW on December 16, 1999. Since going to Germanwings in 2005 it has carried "Berlin Bearbus" advertising for the Berlin-Schönefeld airport.

**Airbus A319-112**, 1016th A319/320/321, built in 1999. D-AKNI was delivered to its first owner, Eurowings, in May 1999, transferred to Germanwings in October 2002, and painted with "Hamburg Shopper" advertising in February 2007.

The vacation airline Hapag-Lloyd, with its low-cost branch HLX, also had several striking airplanes in its fleet. The two airlines joined at the end of 2006 in TUIfly, which has happily continued the tradition of advertising logos.

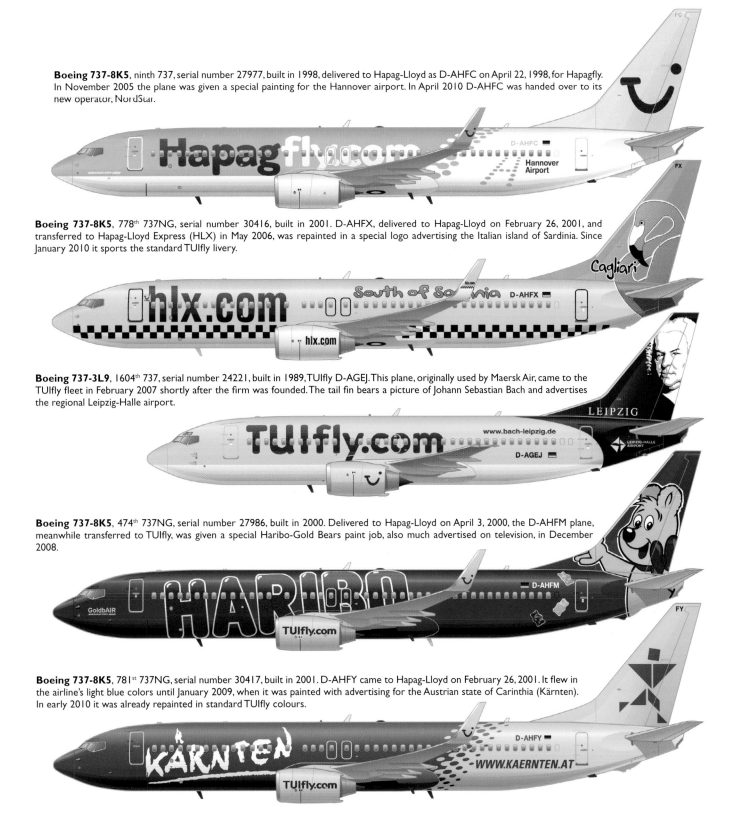

**Boeing 737-8K5**, ninth 737, serial number 27977, built in 1998, delivered to Hapag-Lloyd as D-AHFC on April 22, 1998, for Hapagfly. In November 2005 the plane was given a special painting for the Hannover airport. In April 2010 D-AHFC was handed over to its new operator, NordStar.

**Boeing 737-8K5**, 778th 737NG, serial number 30416, built in 2001. D-AHFX, delivered to Hapag-Lloyd on February 26, 2001, and transferred to Hapag-Lloyd Express (HLX) in May 2006, was repainted in a special logo advertising the Italian island of Sardinia. Since January 2010 it sports the standard TUIfly livery.

**Boeing 737-3L9**, 1604th 737, serial number 24221, built in 1989, TUIfly D-AGEJ. This plane, originally used by Maersk Air, came to the TUIfly fleet in February 2007 shortly after the firm was founded. The tail fin bears a picture of Johann Sebastian Bach and advertises the regional Leipzig-Halle airport.

**Boeing 737-8K5**, 474th 737NG, serial number 27986, built in 2000. Delivered to Hapag-Lloyd on April 3, 2000, the D-AHFM plane, meanwhile transferred to TUIfly, was given a special Haribo-Gold Bears paint job, also much advertised on television, in December 2008.

**Boeing 737-8K5**, 781st 737NG, serial number 30417, built in 2001. D-AHFY came to Hapag-Lloyd on February 26, 2001. It flew in the airline's light blue colors until January 2009, when it was painted with advertising for the Austrian state of Carinthia (Kärnten). In early 2010 it was already repainted in standard TUIfly colours.

# Iberia

Iberia's paint is colorful even without advertising, or better, strikingly colorful. The management probably thinks so, or nearly, for the airline generally avoids specially composed flying advertisements with few exceptions. At the end of 1998 five planes were decorated with Christmas greetings: one 747, one A340, one A300, and two MD-87s; in 2007 an A319 was given a retro paint job, and since 2009 an older A320 serves the "Oneworld" airline union.

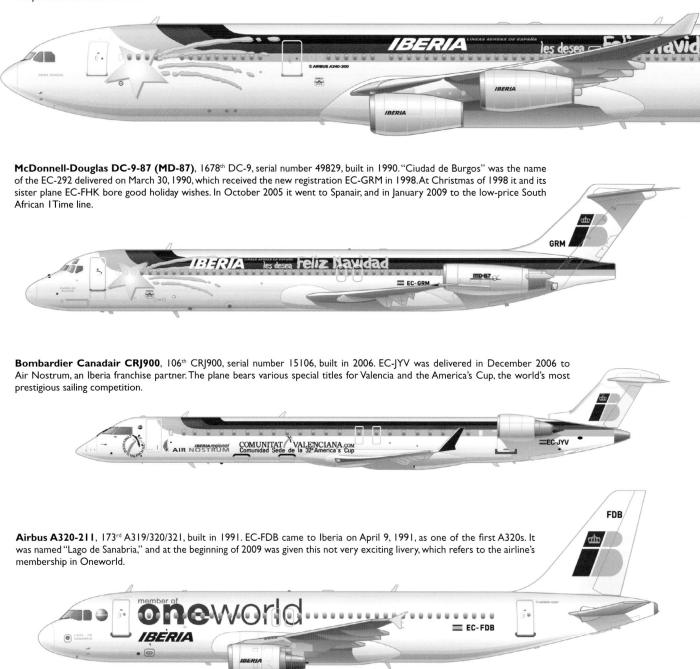

**Airbus A340-313**, 145th A330/340, built in 1996. Delivered to Iberia on September 13, 1996, and named "Rosa Chacel," EC-GJT was given a special Christmas livery toward the end of 1998.

**McDonnell-Douglas DC-9-87 (MD-87)**, 1678th DC-9, serial number 49829, built in 1990. "Ciudad de Burgos" was the name of the EC-292 delivered on March 30, 1990, which received the new registration EC-GRM in 1998. At Christmas of 1998 it and its sister plane EC-FHK bore good holiday wishes. In October 2005 it went to Spanair, and in January 2009 to the low-price South African 1Time line.

**Bombardier Canadair CRJ900**, 106th CRJ900, serial number 15106, built in 2006. EC-JYV was delivered in December 2006 to Air Nostrum, an Iberia franchise partner. The plane bears various special titles for Valencia and the America's Cup, the world's most prestigious sailing competition.

**Airbus A320-211**, 173rd A319/320/321, built in 1991. EC-FDB came to Iberia on April 9, 1991, as one of the first A320s. It was named "Lago de Sanabria," and at the beginning of 2009 was given this not very exciting livery, which refers to the airline's membership in Oneworld.

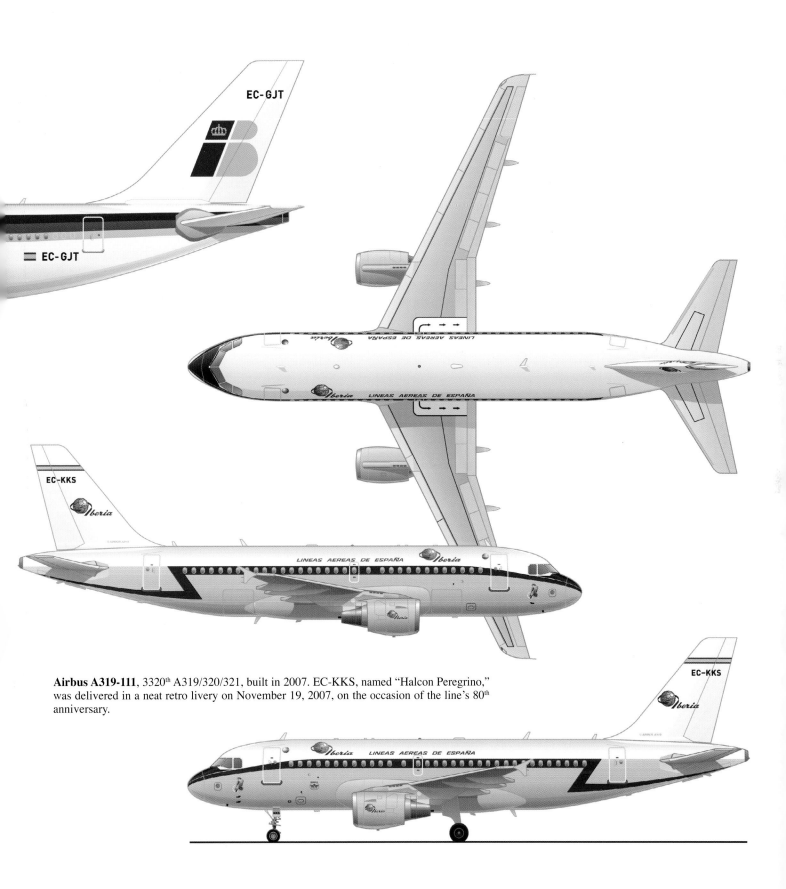

**Airbus A319-111**, 3320th A319/320/321, built in 2007. EC-KKS, named "Halcon Peregrino," was delivered in a neat retro livery on November 19, 2007, on the occasion of the line's 80th anniversary.

EC-GJT

EC-GJT

EC-KKS

EC-KKS

# Japan Airlines

The Japanese flag carrier has a long tradition of special paint jobs. The Boeing 747 in particular, as the line's flagship, was and still is frequently decorated with more or less striking designs. Several examples are given here, for showing all individual JAL planes with special painting or names would explode this book. In 1990 JAL changed its basic livery to an almost completely white scheme with the traditional red crane at the rear and a gray and red stripe at the front. In 2003 another change took place and the crane was replaced by a new logo, with a silver-rimmed red rising sun. At the same time the fuselage color, snowy white until then, was replaced by a broken white. In 1994 JA8111 was the first plane to receive a color scheme called "Super Resort Express." After that several other planes, usually older Boeing 747s and DC-10s used on vacation flights, were given the same livery with lilac, yellow, and later pink variations.

**McDonnell Douglas DC-10-40**, 304th DC-10, serial number 47822, built in 1979. JA8539, delivered to Japan Airlines on January 7, 1980, was passed on to Japan Air Charter (JAZ), one of JAL's many branches, in 1992. From 1998 to 2000 it flew as Super Resort Express, then passed into the hands of JALways and was named "Reso'cha," but retained the violet flower and bird decorations. In November 2003, barely 24 years old, she was taken out of service.

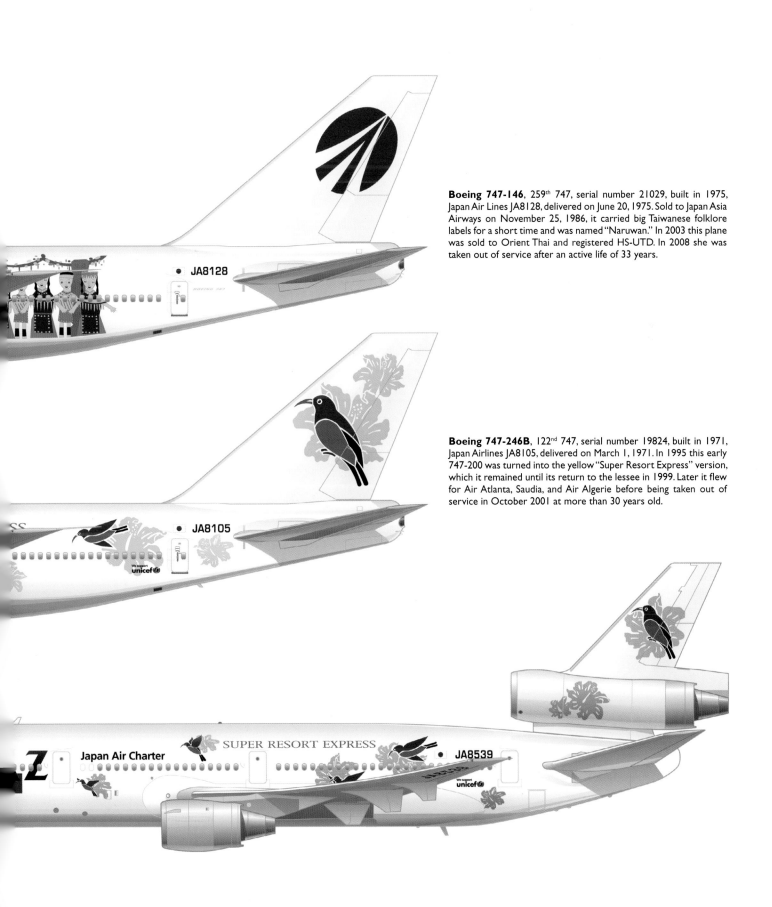

**Boeing 747-146**, 259th 747, serial number 21029, built in 1975, Japan Air Lines JA8128, delivered on June 20, 1975. Sold to Japan Asia Airways on November 25, 1986, it carried big Taiwanese folklore labels for a short time and was named "Naruwan." In 2003 this plane was sold to Orient Thai and registered HS-UTD. In 2008 she was taken out of service after an active life of 33 years.

**Boeing 747-246B**, 122nd 747, serial number 19824, built in 1971, Japan Airlines JA8105, delivered on March 1, 1971. In 1995 this early 747-200 was turned into the yellow "Super Resort Express" version, which it remained until its return to the lessee in 1999. Later it flew for Air Atlanta, Saudia, and Air Algerie before being taken out of service in October 2001 at more than 30 years old.

# Japan Airlines

JAL's "Super Resort Express" flew until 1999-2000; then the Boeing 747-200, 747-300, and DC-10 planes were renamed "Reso'cha," and some were passed on to branch lines. Many acquired a new look, but most of the vacation planes kept the flower patterns that they had borne since the mid-nineties.

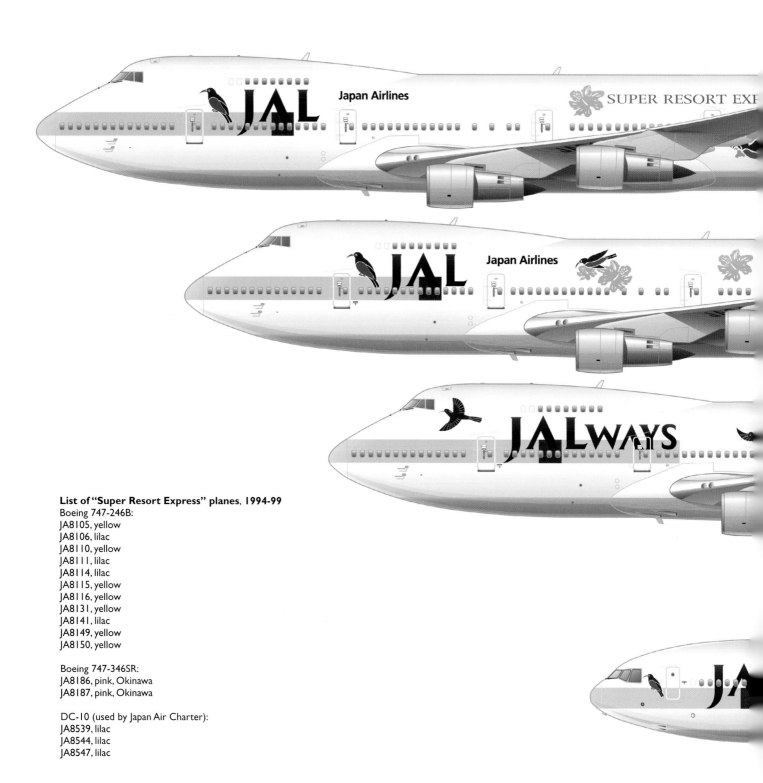

**List of "Super Resort Express" planes, 1994-99**
Boeing 747-246B:
JA8105, yellow
JA8106, lilac
JA8110, yellow
JA8111, lilac
JA8114, lilac
JA8115, yellow
JA8116, yellow
JA8131, yellow
JA8141, lilac
JA8149, yellow
JA8150, yellow

Boeing 747-346SR:
JA8186, pink, Okinawa
JA8187, pink, Okinawa

DC-10 (used by Japan Air Charter):
JA8539, lilac
JA8544, lilac
JA8547, lilac

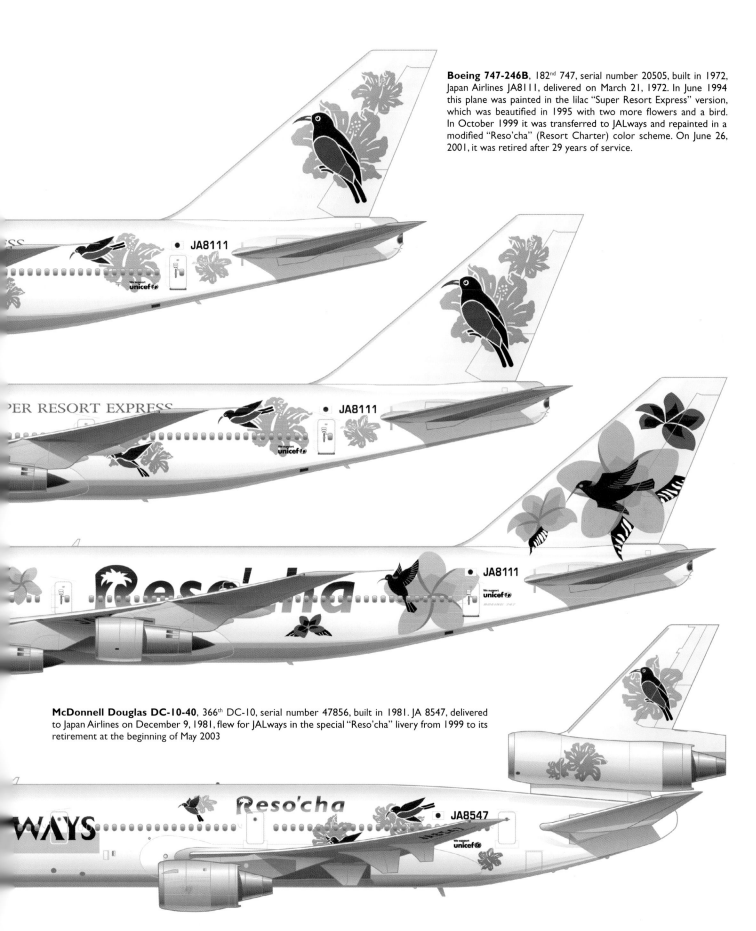

**Boeing 747-246B**, 182$^{nd}$ 747, serial number 20505, built in 1972, Japan Airlines JA8111, delivered on March 21, 1972. In June 1994 this plane was painted in the lilac "Super Resort Express" version, which was beautified in 1995 with two more flowers and a bird. In October 1999 it was transferred to JALways and repainted in a modified "Reso'cha" (Resort Charter) color scheme. On June 26, 2001, it was retired after 29 years of service.

**McDonnell Douglas DC-10-40**, 366$^{th}$ DC-10, serial number 47856, built in 1981. JA 8547, delivered to Japan Airlines on December 9, 1981, flew for JALways in the special "Reso'cha" livery from 1999 to its retirement at the beginning of May 2003

# Japan Airlines

**Boeing 747-346 SR**, 692nd 747, serial number 23967, built in 1987, Japan Airlines JA8183, delivered on December 10, 1987. In February 1999 the former short-flight planes were refitted as 747-346 long-flight versions. As of mid-2001 they flew in another version of the "Reso'cha" vacation flight livery. In the summer of 2007 it and its remaining sister planes were repainted in the new standard JAL livery. Thus, the time of the series of colorful Japan Airlines vacation planes ended for the time being.

**Boeing 747-346 SR**, 694th 747, serial number 24018, built in 1988, Japan Airlines JA 8186, delivered on February 9, 1988. Painted as "Super Resort Express Okinawa" in 1997; the Okinawa title was removed in 1999 and the short-flight plane was refitted as a long-flight 747-346. In March 2000 it was given a new "Reso'cha" logo, a sort of successor to the "Super Resort Express." Transferred to JALways in September 2002, it was painted in the new standard JAL livery five years later. In September 2008 the plane was sold to Orient Thai and reregistered HS-UTS, the first duty for her new owners being Hadj pilgrim flights under the logo of Garuda Indonesia. Months later the aircraft went to the Nigerian start-up Max Air.

# Japan Airlines

In 2001 the firm celebrated its fiftieth anniversary in grand style; interestingly enough, JAL also celebrated Walt Disney's 100th birthday. For this occasion six Boeing 747-400s, five of them inland planes, were decorated for a year with various Disney World motifs. Shortly thereafter, in 2003, the corporate identity was changed. The traditional crane was replaced by a new logo, a rising red sun with a silver border. At the same time the formerly snow-white fuselage color was replaced by a broken, slightly rose-colored white.

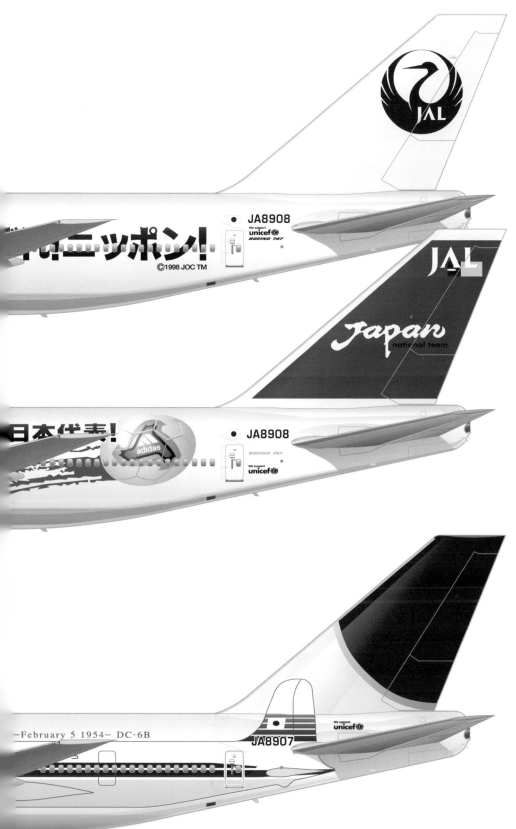

**Boeing 747-446D**, 978th 747, serial number 26352, built in 1993. Delivered on June 1, 1993, with JA8908 registration. In 2000 this plane flew with big "Sydney Olympics Official Airliner" lettering for the Olympic Games in Sydney. In 2001, for the airline's 50th anniversary, the plane bore a Disney Dream Express logo on a white background. At the beginning of 2002 it was given another special paint job for the world soccer championship, which took place in Japan and Korea that year.

**Boeing 747-446D**, 963rd 747, serial number 26351, built in 1993. Delivered to Japan Airlines on March 2, 1993, with JA8907 registration, it was redone with striking labels to honor Japanese baseball star Hideki Matsui. Right after that it received another special paint job for the 50th anniversary of the Okinawa route, much like that which was applied to its sister plane JA8906 for the 50th anniversary of the Hawaii route.

# Japan Airlines

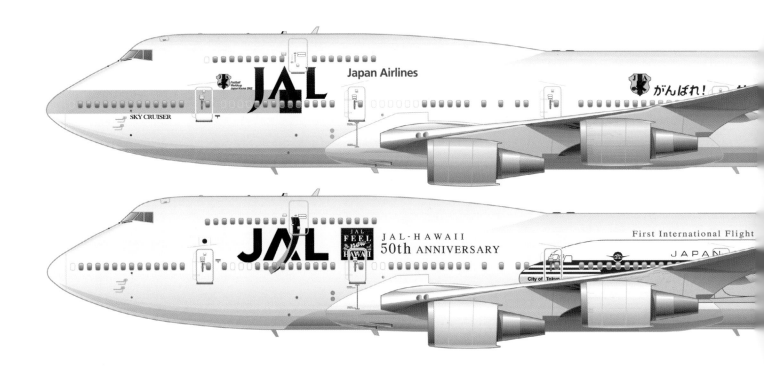

**Boeing 767-346**, 905th 767, serial number 33493, built in 2003. JA604J was delivered to Japan Airlines on April 22, 2003, and was one of the first planes to bear the new livery. In February 2009 it was given the special "Oneworld" logo. JAL is one of the last customers to order this no longer young type of airplane.

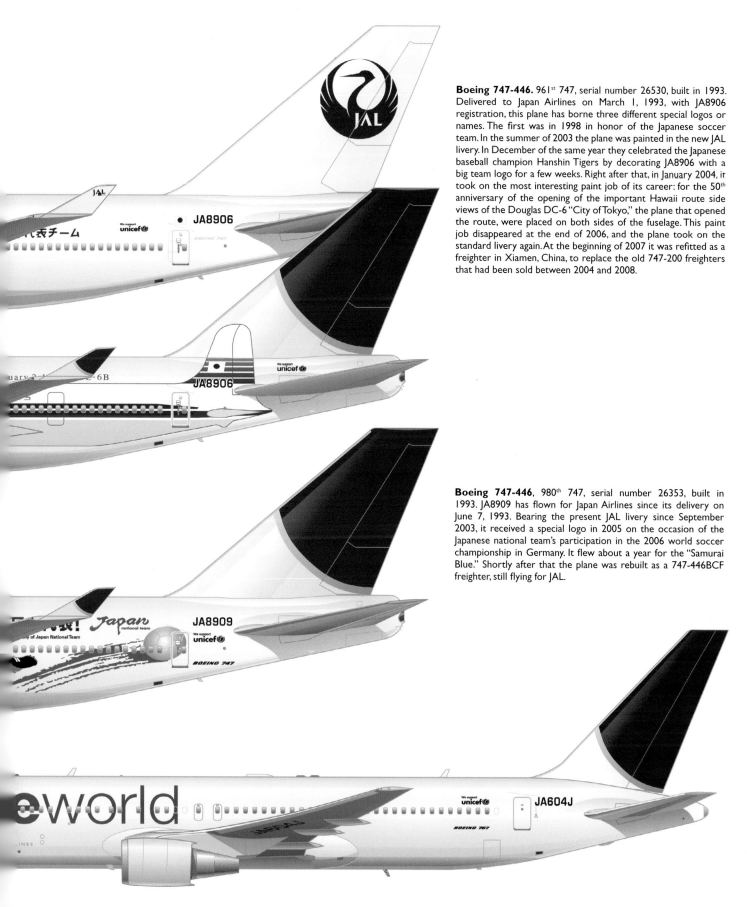

**Boeing 747-446.** 961st 747, serial number 26530, built in 1993. Delivered to Japan Airlines on March 1, 1993, with JA8906 registration, this plane has borne three different special logos or names. The first was in 1998 in honor of the Japanese soccer team. In the summer of 2003 the plane was painted in the new JAL livery. In December of the same year they celebrated the Japanese baseball champion Hanshin Tigers by decorating JA8906 with a big team logo for a few weeks. Right after that, in January 2004, it took on the most interesting paint job of its career: for the 50th anniversary of the opening of the important Hawaii route side views of the Douglas DC-6 "City of Tokyo," the plane that opened the route, were placed on both sides of the fuselage. This paint job disappeared at the end of 2006, and the plane took on the standard livery again. At the beginning of 2007 it was refitted as a freighter in Xiamen, China, to replace the old 747-200 freighters that had been sold between 2004 and 2008.

**Boeing 747-446**, 980th 747, serial number 26353, built in 1993. JA8909 has flown for Japan Airlines since its delivery on June 7, 1993. Bearing the present JAL livery since September 2003, it received a special logo in 2005 on the occasion of the Japanese national team's participation in the 2006 world soccer championship in Germany. It flew about a year for the "Samurai Blue." Shortly after that the plane was rebuilt as a 747-446BCF freighter, still flying for JAL.

# Japan Airlines

"Yokoso! Japan" is the name of the campaign begun at the start of 2005 to lure more people to the Land of the Rising Sun. A series of planes bore various versions of the appropriate invitation.

By the end of the first decade of the new millennium JAL had run into crisis, made worse by the recession of 2008/09.

Near bankruptcy, the air line is forced to shrink dramatically. The saddest side effect, at least for aviation enthusiasts, will be the short term removal of the once great Boeing 747 fleet. If JAL's transition into a mid-sized twinjet operator will be successful, is doubtful. Especially when noticing that the international competition is beginning to fly the A380 to Japan, something JAL has no competitive aircraft to place against.

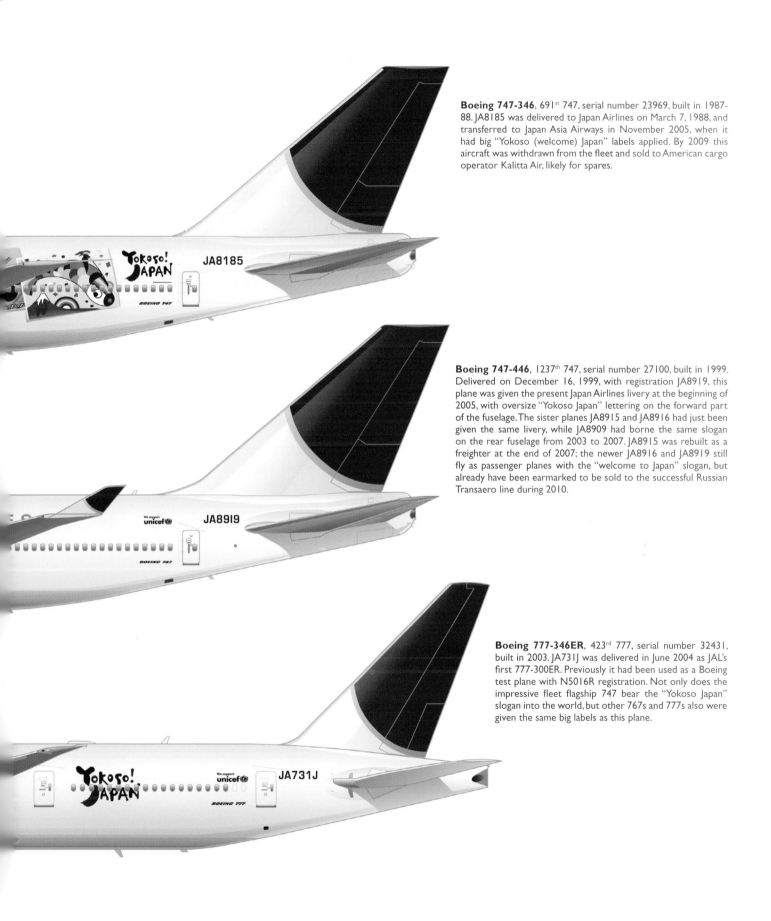

**Boeing 747-346**, 691st 747, serial number 23969, built in 1987-88. JA8185 was delivered to Japan Airlines on March 7, 1988, and transferred to Japan Asia Airways in November 2005, when it had big "Yokoso (welcome) Japan" labels applied. By 2009 this aircraft was withdrawn from the fleet and sold to American cargo operator Kalitta Air, likely for spares.

**Boeing 747-446**, 1237th 747, serial number 27100, built in 1999. Delivered on December 16, 1999, with registration JA8919, this plane was given the present Japan Airlines livery at the beginning of 2005, with oversize "Yokoso Japan" lettering on the forward part of the fuselage. The sister planes JA8915 and JA8916 had just been given the same livery, while JA8909 had borne the same slogan on the rear fuselage from 2003 to 2007. JA8915 was rebuilt as a freighter at the end of 2007; the newer JA8916 and JA8919 still fly as passenger planes with the "welcome to Japan" slogan, but already have been earmarked to be sold to the successful Russian Transaero line during 2010.

**Boeing 777-346ER**, 423rd 777, serial number 32431, built in 2003. JA731J was delivered in June 2004 as JAL's first 777-300ER. Previously it had been used as a Boeing test plane with N5016R registration. Not only does the impressive fleet flagship 747 bear the "Yokoso Japan" slogan into the world, but other 767s and 777s also were given the same big labels as this plane.

# Japan Airlines

Japan Airlines uses their airplanes for a variety of messages, advertisements, or self promotions. Large airplanes have carried labels advertising the world-famous Japanese toy manufacturer Tamagochi since 2006, and since 2007 several of the fleet's approximately 200 planes have borne environmental slogans.

**Boeing 777-246**, 86th 777, serial number 27651, built in 1997. Delivered on April 21, 1997, with JA8984 registration, this Triple Seven flies mainly on short and medium routes. In 2003 it was given the present JAL livery, in 2007 it became a "Sakitoku" advertiser, and in 2008 the tail fin was painted green, proclaiming an ecological message called "Eco Sky."

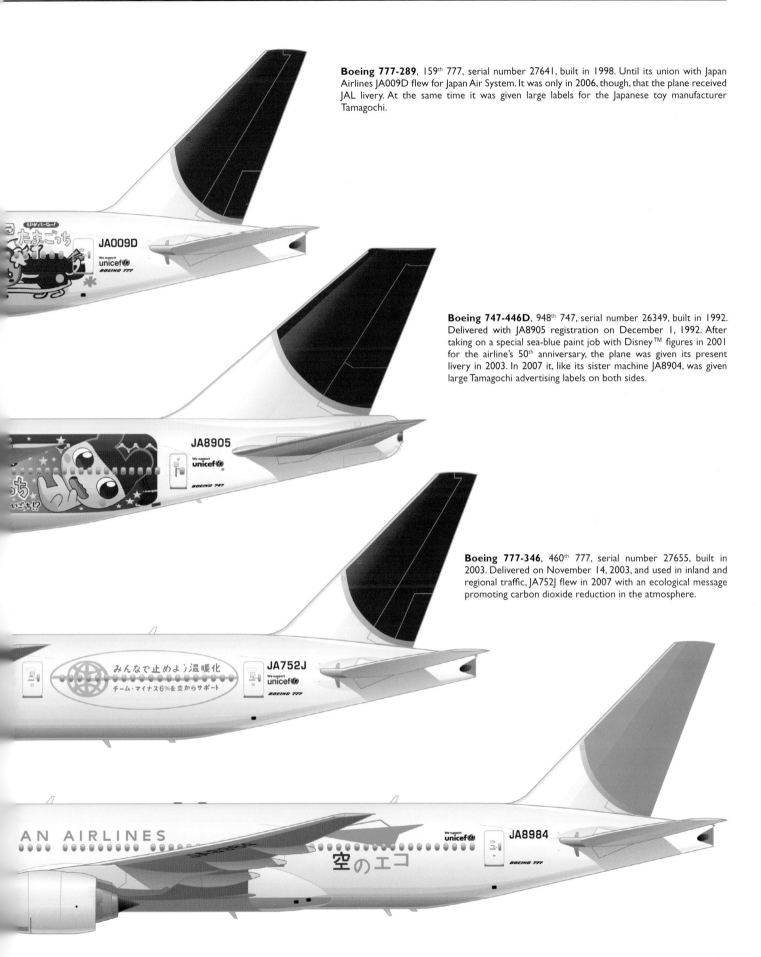

**Boeing 777-289**, 159th 777, serial number 27641, built in 1998. Until its union with Japan Airlines JA009D flew for Japan Air System. It was only in 2006, though, that the plane received JAL livery. At the same time it was given large labels for the Japanese toy manufacturer Tamagochi.

**Boeing 747-446D**, 948th 747, serial number 26349, built in 1992. Delivered with JA8905 registration on December 1, 1992. After taking on a special sea-blue paint job with Disney™ figures in 2001 for the airline's 50th anniversary, the plane was given its present livery in 2003. In 2007 it, like its sister machine JA8904, was given large Tamagochi advertising labels on both sides.

**Boeing 777-346**, 460th 777, serial number 27655, built in 2003. Delivered on November 14, 2003, and used in inland and regional traffic, JA752J flew in 2007 with an ecological message promoting carbon dioxide reduction in the atmosphere.

# Japan Airlines Cargo

There were also special paint jobs among the 747 cargo fleet of Japan Airlines. In the late 1980s, for example, several planes bore large registration numbers on their tail fins in place of the usual crane. In 1996 the cargo department was renamed "Super Logistics," and the planes of that part of the fleet that flew to China were given their own tail fin design. Since 2002 this has been reversed. The present-day cargo fleet consists of two silver 747-400F planes and a series of repainted former 747-400 passenger liners with standard livery. But their days in JAL service are numbered, as in the wake of the crisis the airline is about to close down its cargo arm completely by the end of 2010.

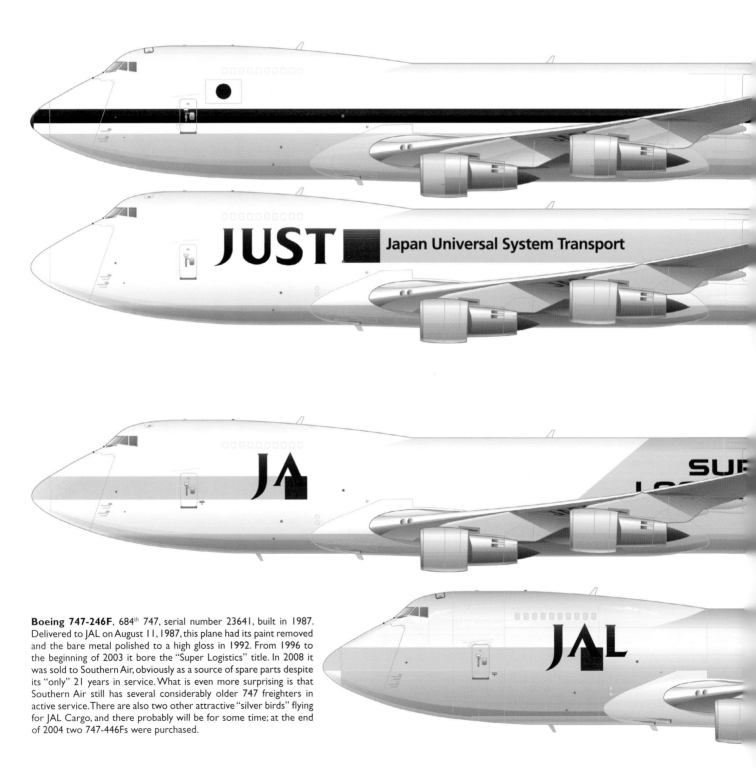

**Boeing 747-246F**, 684th 747, serial number 23641, built in 1987. Delivered to JAL on August 11, 1987, this plane had its paint removed and the bare metal polished to a high gloss in 1992. From 1996 to the beginning of 2003 it bore the "Super Logistics" title. In 2008 it was sold to Southern Air, obviously as a source of spare parts despite its "only" 21 years in service. What is even more surprising is that Southern Air still has several considerably older 747 freighters in active service. There are also two other attractive "silver birds" flying for JAL Cargo, and there probably will be for some time; at the end of 2004 two 747-446Fs were purchased.

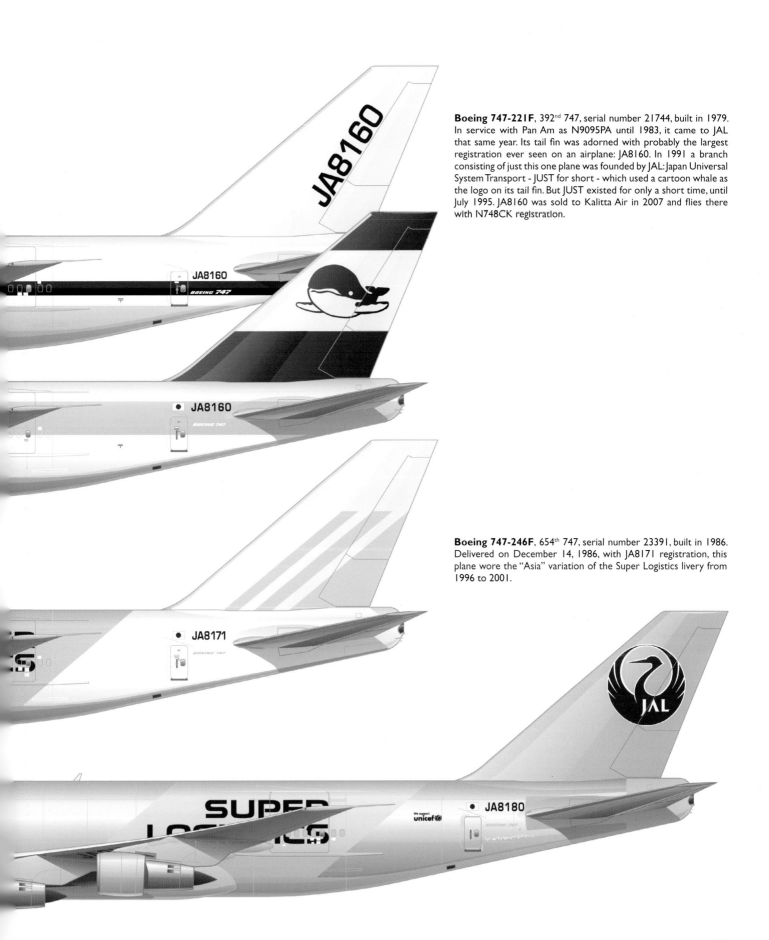

**Boeing 747-221F**, 392nd 747, serial number 21744, built in 1979. In service with Pan Am as N9095PA until 1983, it came to JAL that same year. Its tail fin was adorned with probably the largest registration ever seen on an airplane: JA8160. In 1991 a branch consisting of just this one plane was founded by JAL: Japan Universal System Transport - JUST for short - which used a cartoon whale as the logo on its tail fin. But JUST existed for only a short time, until July 1995. JA8160 was sold to Kalitta Air in 2007 and flies there with N748CK registration.

**Boeing 747-246F**, 654th 747, serial number 23391, built in 1986. Delivered on December 14, 1986, with JA8171 registration, this plane wore the "Asia" variation of the Super Logistics livery from 1996 to 2001.

# KLM

KLM, one of the world's oldest airlines, is unusual among high-ranking international airlines in not having used a single plane until 2009 with a complete special paint job. Yet there have been several interestingly painted exceptions, the first of which is shown here in all its glory.

**Boeing 747-206B**, 170th 747, serial number 20427, built in 1971. PH-BUG, the last of seven planes forming KLM's first group of 747s, was named "Orinoco," and was used along with the Venezuelan Viasa until 1975; it bore a very unusual paint job. Very normal on the left side in KLM livery originating in the 1960s, it bore the full livery of Viasa on the right side. In 1975 it finally acquired the new long-term KLM livery. The upper deck was finally modified with ten windows on each side. At the end of 1991 the plane was taken out of service, then was sold to Corsair, where she flew another six years. Thirty years old, she was finally mothballed after the events of 9/11/2001 and then broken up at Chateauroux, France, in 2002.

# KLM

The first KLM planes that deviated from the normal livery were the first two full-freighters, two former passenger liners rebuilt in 1997 that were replaced by factory-new 747-400Fs in 2002. At the end of 2002 KLM began a large-scale advertising campaign called "The world is just a click away!" to promote internet booking. In the course of this campaign several planes were labeled with this slogan, along with the trade mark, a flying swan. Only at the beginning of 2009 did the first really special paint job make its debut in the KLM fleet: a Boeing 737-800 in retro livery for the firm's 90th anniversary.

**Boeing 737-306**, 1275th 737, serial number 23527, built in 1986. Delivered to KLM on September 30, 1986, this plane was given the name of the seafarer and explorer Willem Barentsz. In 2003-04 it bore the striking labels of "The world is just a click away!" internet campaign. PH-BDA was finally retired in the summer of 2009.

**Boeing 747-206B/SUD/SF**, 271st 747, serial number 21110, built in 1975. The delivery date of PH-BUH, named after KLM's founder, Dr. Albert Piesman, was October 19, 1975. In 1985 the upper deck of the plane was lengthened, which gave it the unusual type numbering of 747-206B/SUD, with SUD standing for "stretched upper deck." In 1997, along with a sister plane, it was converted to a freighter, and the type designation had SF for "special freighter" added. On this occasion the painting was modified and a very large slogan was added. In 2002 the aging freighter, still apparently in good condition, was sold, for as we went to press it was still, after 33 years in service, active for the American firm of Southern Air.

**Boeing 747-406M**, 1302nd 747, serial number 30455, built in 2002. PH-BFY, named "Johannesburg," is the last passenger 747 delivered to KLM, being sent to Amsterdam on April 10, 2002. Shortly after that it was given large Internet labels which remained in place until October 2004. Since 2005 the plane has been flying in the new KLM livery.

**Boeing 737-806**, 198th Next Generation 737, serial number 29131, built in 1999. PH-BXA was delivered on February 25, 1999, and named "Zwaan" (swan). For the firm's 90th anniversary in 2009 the plane was given a handsome retro livery in the style of the early sixties.

# Korean Air

Korean Air is the national airline of South Korea. The elegant light blue livery of their planes was already introduced in 1985, and almost 25 years later it still looks up-to-date - proof of a good design. On the occasion of the 2002 world soccer championship, which took place in South Korea and Japan, three of the fleet's planes, a Boeing 747-400, a 777-200, and an A330-300, were fitted with large special markings. Today, in 2010, an A300, A330, and a 747-400 of Korean Air bear special paint jobs.

**Boeing 777-2B5ER**, 356th 777, serial number 27949, built in 2001. Delivered on September 28, 2001, HL 7589 soon received a special paint job as advertising for the 2002 world soccer championship. As with the 747 shown above, it gained a new title afterward, in reference to the Asian championship. The special logo was eliminated at the end of 2002.

**Boeing 747-4B5 ER F**, 1350th 747, serial number 33946, built in 2004. The freighter, delivered on August 6, 2004, bore a large label for about a year to identify it as Korean Air's 100th Boeing plane.

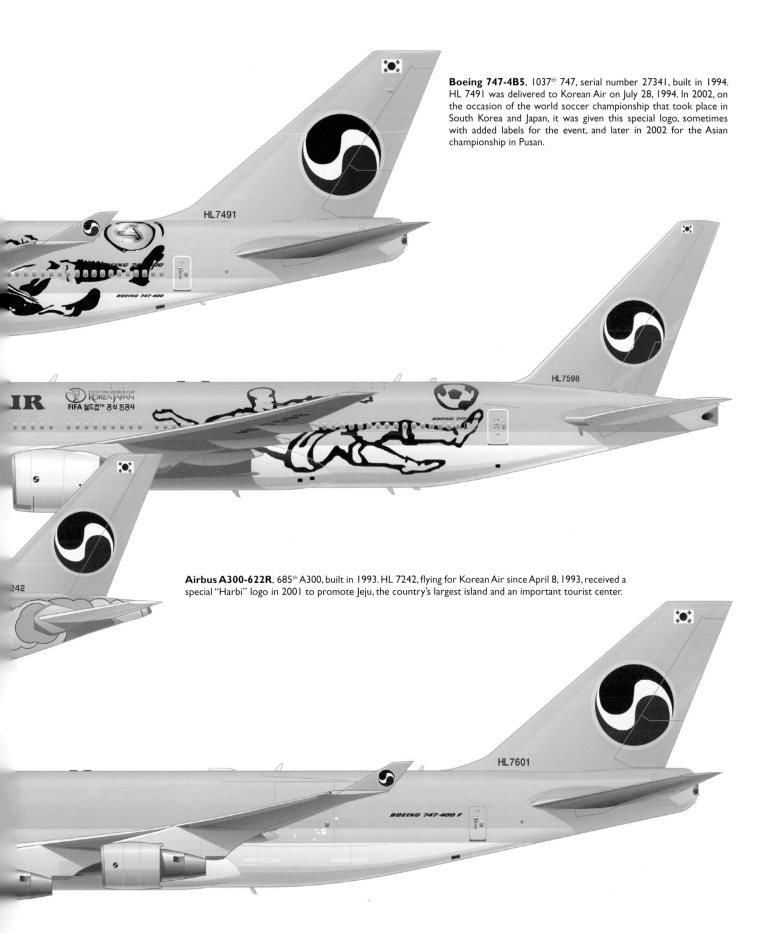

**Boeing 747-4B5**, 1037th 747, serial number 27341, built in 1994. HL 7491 was delivered to Korean Air on July 28, 1994. In 2002, on the occasion of the world soccer championship that took place in South Korea and Japan, it was given this special logo, sometimes with added labels for the event, and later in 2002 for the Asian championship in Pusan.

**Airbus A300-622R**, 685th A300, built in 1993. HL 7242, flying for Korean Air since April 8, 1993, received a special "Harbi" logo in 2001 to promote Jeju, the country's largest island and an important tourist center.

# LTU/Air Berlin

LTU, which was bought in 2007 and then integrated by Air Berlin, also had a few specially painted planes in its fleet. Better known, though, were the A320s decorated with the logos of well-known domestic and foreign soccer teams. Air Berlin has had to date only one plane with a special paint job, a 737-700 in Boeing Dreamliner livery.

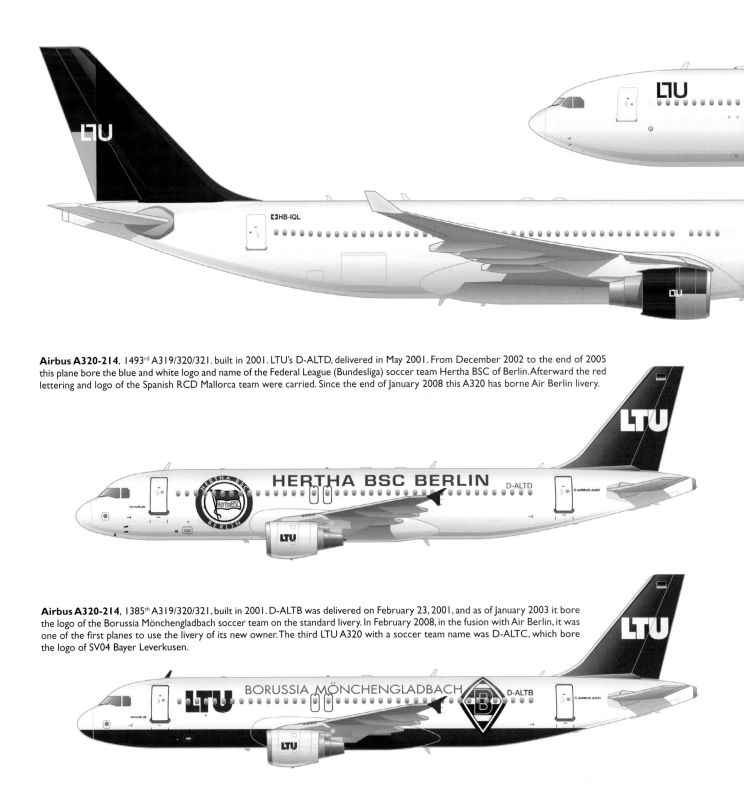

**Airbus A320-214**, 1493rd A319/320/321. built in 2001. LTU's D-ALTD, delivered in May 2001. From December 2002 to the end of 2005 this plane bore the blue and white logo and name of the Federal League (Bundesliga) soccer team Hertha BSC of Berlin. Afterward the red lettering and logo of the Spanish RCD Mallorca team were carried. Since the end of January 2008 this A320 has borne Air Berlin livery.

**Airbus A320-214**, 1385th A319/320/321, built in 2001. D-ALTB was delivered on February 23, 2001, and as of January 2003 it bore the logo of the Borussia Mönchengladbach soccer team on the standard livery. In February 2008, in the fusion with Air Berlin, it was one of the first planes to use the livery of its new owner. The third LTU A320 with a soccer team name was D-ALTC, which bore the logo of SV04 Bayer Leverkusen.

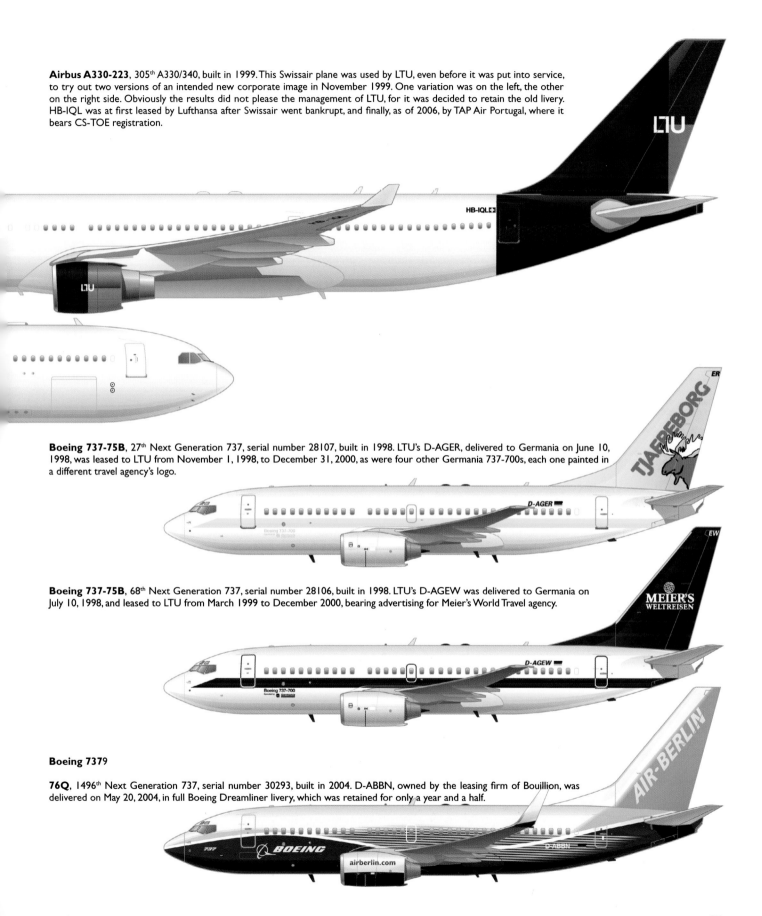

**Airbus A330-223**, 305th A330/340, built in 1999. This Swissair plane was used by LTU, even before it was put into service, to try out two versions of an intended new corporate image in November 1999. One variation was on the left, the other on the right side. Obviously the results did not please the management of LTU, for it was decided to retain the old livery. HB-IQL was at first leased by Lufthansa after Swissair went bankrupt, and finally, as of 2006, by TAP Air Portugal, where it bears CS-TOE registration.

**Boeing 737-75B**, 27th Next Generation 737, serial number 28107, built in 1998. LTU's D-AGER, delivered to Germania on June 10, 1998, was leased to LTU from November 1, 1998, to December 31, 2000, as were four other Germania 737-700s, each one painted in a different travel agency's logo.

**Boeing 737-75B**, 68th Next Generation 737, serial number 28106, built in 1998. LTU's D-AGEW was delivered to Germania on July 10, 1998, and leased to LTU from March 1999 to December 2000, bearing advertising for Meier's World Travel agency.

**Boeing 7379**

**76Q**, 1496th Next Generation 737, serial number 30293, built in 2004. D-ABBN, owned by the leasing firm of Bouillion, was delivered on May 20, 2004, in full Boeing Dreamliner livery, which was retained for only a year and a half.

# Lufthansa

Lufthansa is known for strict procedure with its corporate identity. Playfulness is not practiced by the renowned German airline. Yet there have been a few exceptions to the rule. The best known is the single A321 that was painted in 2005 with a lovely traditional livery for the postwar airline's 50th anniversary, such as the first Boeing 707s were given in the early sixties.

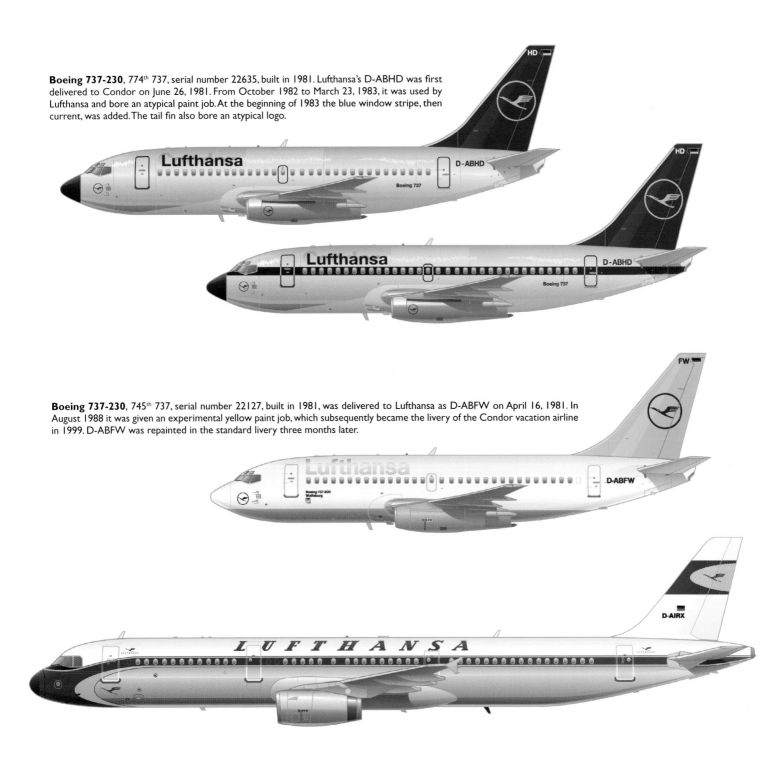

**Boeing 737-230**, 774th 737, serial number 22635, built in 1981. Lufthansa's D-ABHD was first delivered to Condor on June 26, 1981. From October 1982 to March 23, 1983, it was used by Lufthansa and bore an atypical paint job. At the beginning of 1983 the blue window stripe, then current, was added. The tail fin also bore an atypical logo.

**Boeing 737-230**, 745th 737, serial number 22127, built in 1981, was delivered to Lufthansa as D-ABFW on April 16, 1981. In August 1988 it was given an experimental yellow paint job, which subsequently became the livery of the Condor vacation airline in 1999. D-ABFW was repainted in the standard livery three months later.

**Boeing 727-230**, 1021st 727, serial number 20790, built in 1974. Lufthansa's D-ABTI was delivered to Condor on March 19, 1974. From November 8, 1988, to March 8, 1989, it was leased by Lufthansa, but kept the gray fuselage color of Condor, as did a DC 10 also leased from Condor. Whether these planes were used to evaluate the new Lufthansa corporate image is not known.

**Airbus A310-304**, 484th A300/310, built in 1988. This plane was painted at the Airbus works in Toulouse, still with the F-WWCI test registration, in the yellow experimental livery, but this time with blue titles that were easier to read. On November 22, 1988, it was registered as D-AIDB, then given the new livery that had meanwhile been chosen and that it still used twenty years later, and delivered to Lufthansa. D-AIDB did not fly for Lufthansa very long and was sold to the German Air Force on August 14, 1996.

**Airbus A321-131**, 887th A319/320/321, built in 1998. Delivered to Lufthansa with D-AIRX registration on October 1, 1998, it was chosen in 2005 to bear the very attractive anniversary livery for the firm's 50th birthday. It is much like the paint job that was developed around 1960 when the first jet airliners were introduced. The fuselage of the A321 corresponds in its dimensions almost exactly to the Boeing 707 jet pioneer.

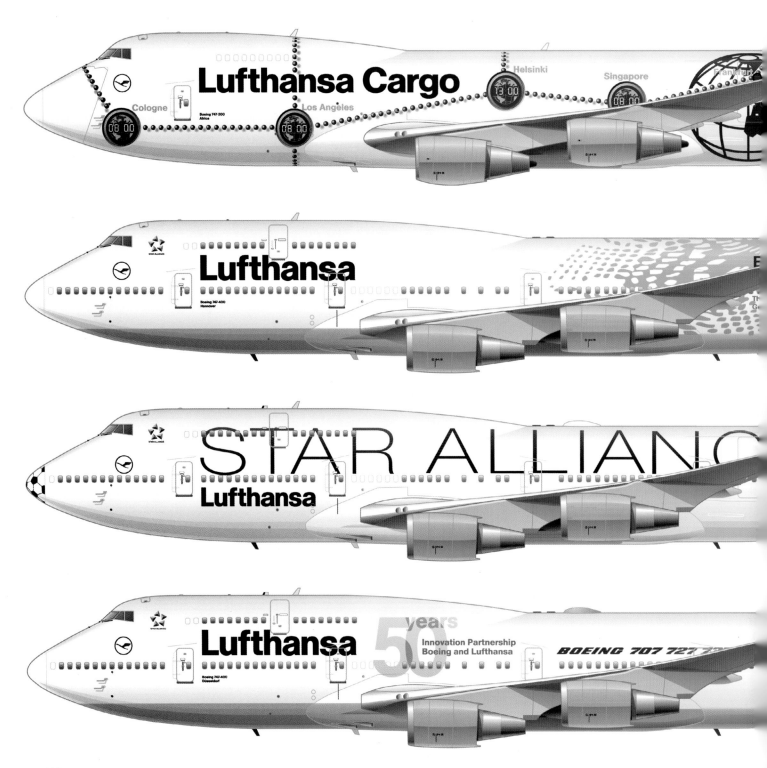

**Boeing 747-230F**, 660th 747, serial number 21621, built in 1986. Delivered to Lufthansa with D-ABZF registration on October 24, 1986, the plane, named "Africa," was painted in an attractive special form called "Service Revolution." At the end of 2001 it was briefly taken out of service and parked in the USA after 11 September. Reactivated in the spring of 2002, its special livery was painted over. In July 2004 the freighter, 18 years old, was finally sold to Air Atlanta and re-registered TF-ARR. Only four months later it went out of control on the runway after a tire blew in Sharjah, United Arab Emirates, and had to be written off. Fortunately, the crew was not harmed in the accident.

**Boeing 747-430**, 847th 747 built, serial number 25046, built in 1991, delivered to Lufthansa as D-ABVK on April 19, 1991. On the occasion of the "Expo 2000" fair in Hannover the plane was fittingly given the same name, plus an "Expo 2000" logo extending along both sides.

**Boeing 747-430 M**, 856th 747, serial number 25047, built in 1991, delivered to Lufthansa as D-ABTH on June 5, 1991. The plane, named "Duisburg," was originally built as a Combi version with a freight door, and bore the "Star Alliance" logo from 2003 to November 2008. In December 2005 a big internet antenna was attached to the upper side. At the beginning of 2006 the plane's nose was painted to represent a soccer ball, a clever idea for the world soccer championship of 2006 in Germany that was applied to other Lufthansa planes until 2007.

**Boeing 747-430**, 845th 747, serial number 25045, built 1991. Delivered on 4 April 1991 and christenend „Düsseldorf" after one of the country´s most important cities, this airliner was chosen to participate in the celebration party on the occasion of the 50th anniversary of the successful Lufthansa-Boeing partnership in May 2010, a partnership leading to such important types as the Boeing 737, 747-200 freighter and 747-8 for which the German carrier became the influential launch customer. D-ABVH received fitting titles which no one could miss.

# Malaysia Airlines

The Malaysian flag carrier, existing since 1947, was given its present name only in 1987. In 2009 it has run a fleet of about 90 planes, with Boeing 747-400, 777-200ER, Airbus A330, and Boeing 737-400 and -800, plus 747-400 and 747-200 freighters. Only on one occasion were three of the line's planes given special paint jobs. They went over very successfully and doubtless rank among the world's loveliest "colorful birds."

**Boeing 747-4H6**, 997th 747, serial number 25701, built in 1993. 9M-MPD, delivered on October 5, 1993, and named "Seremban," was given an attention-getting new special livery called "Hibiscus" when it was fitted with new seats. This very attractive paint job, also applied to sister plane 9M-MPB, was unfortunately overpainted with the standard livery three years later.

**Boeing 777-2H6 ER**, 84th 777, serial number 28411, built in 1997, was delivered to Malaysian Airlines on July 29, 1997. For the same reason as the 747 shown above it was given this very attractive special logo called "Heliconia" in 2005, which was overpainted with the normal livery in 2008. For many air travel fans this was the loveliest 777 ever.

**Boeing 767-31A ER**, 415th 767, serial number 26469, built in 1992. PH-MCL was delivered to Martinair on February 12, 1992, and named "Queen Beatrix." After it had borne an advertisement for the Fox Kids cartoon characters in 2002-03 it was painted in retro style in 2008 for the line's 50th anniversary.

# Martinair

Martinair, a private international airline from Holland, was founded in 1958. Today it runs a small fleet of MD-11 and Boeing 747-400 freighters, as well as Boeing 767 passenger planes. Martinair now fully belongs to KLM and has taken over the Dutch flag carrier's 747-400 freighter fleet by the beginning of 2010.

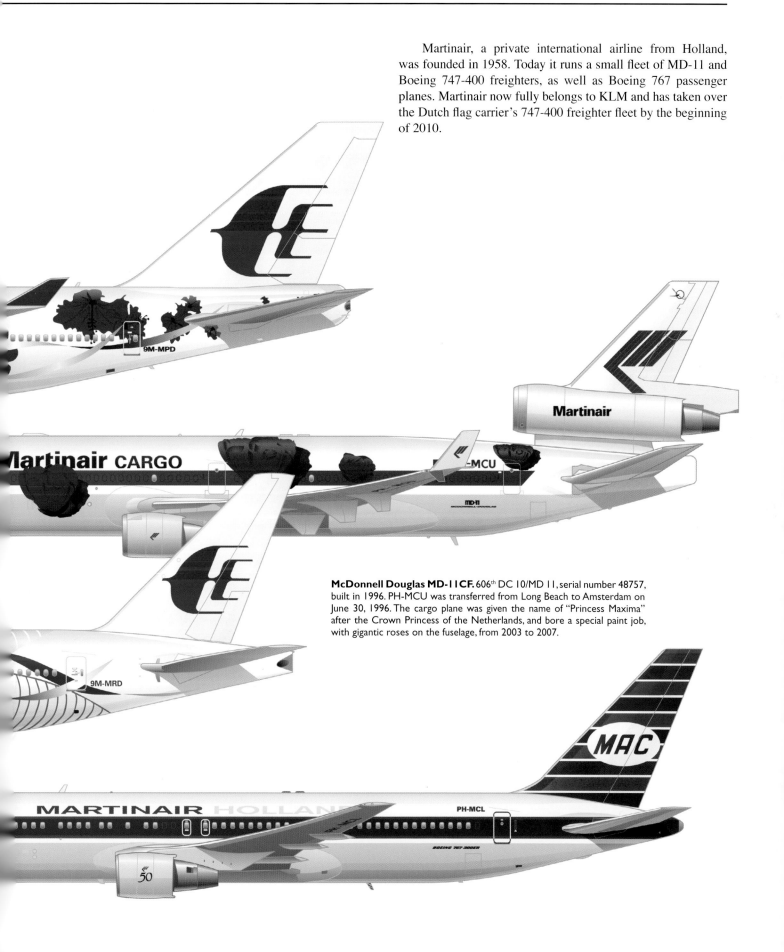

**McDonnell Douglas MD-11CF.** 606th DC 10/MD 11, serial number 48757, built in 1996. PH-MCU was transferred from Long Beach to Amsterdam on June 30, 1996. The cargo plane was given the name of "Princess Maxima" after the Crown Princess of the Netherlands, and bore a special paint job, with gigantic roses on the fuselage, from 2003 to 2007.

# Northwest Airlines

One of the Big Five among U.S. airlines, Northwest was a pioneer of the Pacific routes. In 2008 its merger with Delta Airlines was made known. This took place during 2009, and a tradition-rich name disappeared from the skies when during 2010 the last red-tailed planes were over-painted with Delta's less distinctive colours. Special paintings on Northwest planes have been rare in view of the line's size. In the mid-nineties, despite the attractive livery with a red upper fuselage introduced just a few years before, a few very dull gray experimental paint jobs were tried, but their acceptance was fortunately declined.

**McDonnell Douglas DC-10-30**, 336th DC-10, serial number 47844, built in 1980. This ex-Varig plane was bought by Northwest on December 30, 1997, and registered N237NW. It flew until April 2000 in these colors, indicating the very close relationship of this airline with KLM. At the beginning of 2007 it was taken out of service; since 2008 it has flown for World Airways as N136WA.

**McDonnell Douglas DC-9-51**, 990th DC-9, serial number 48149, built in 1981. Delivered to Republic Airlines on April 17, 1981, N787NC came to Northwest Airlines in a 1986 merger. In 1994-95 a color variation with a light gray fuselage was tried out on it. At the beginning of 2009 this plane, despite its age, was one of the first to be given a Delta Air Lines livery.

**Boeing 747-251B**, 378th 747, serial number 21707, built in 1979. Delivered on June 17, 1979, N625US was chartered for 1991 flight sof U.S. "Desert Storm" troops. It was given huge yellow ribbons, the traditional symbol by which America remembers fighting U.S. soldiers. In 1992 the whole fleet received labels with the logo of the Northwest-KLM alliance. For the 50th anniversary of the first trans-pacific flight all the planes were given appropriate labels, placed on the left front and right rear of the fuselage. N625US was taken out of service in October 2003.

**Boeing 757-251**, 196th 757, serial number 24265, built in 1988. N534US was delivered to Northwest Airlines on October 21, 1988. From 1995 to 1997 this plane was used to test a simplified livery. In 1996 the names were modified as shown here. Fortunately, nothing came of this simple color scheme; the corporate identity was changed only in 2003, and then radically.

# Northwest Airlines

In 1999 Northwest Airlines bought four used 747-200 freighters to add to its fleet of 747s bought new in the seventies and eighties. Since the Northwest Cargo planes normally have an unpainted metal fuselage, and sandblasting and polishing the "new" freighters presumably was difficult, it was decided to give these four freighters different special paint jobs. Delta closed down the Northwest cargo arm at the end of 2009.

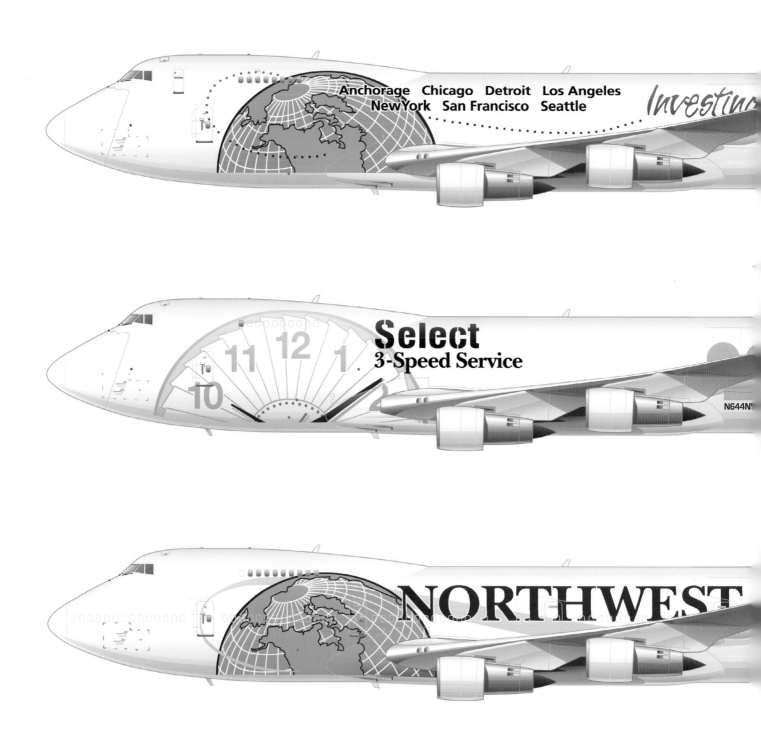

**Boeing 747-249F**, 458th 747, serial number 22245, built in 1980. The former Flying Tigers plane has flown since May 1999 as Northwest Cargo's N643NW. Until the beginning of 2008 it bore a special livery, as the names indicate, referring particularly to Pacific routes. Since March 2008 it has borne the standard NWA livery. Like all of Northwest's 747-200 freighters, this aircraft was stored towards the end of 2009.

**Boeing 747-212F**, 710th 747, serial number 24177, built in 1988. This plane, originally flying for Singapore Airlines as 9V-SKQ, was obtained on October 29, 1999, and gained N644NW registration plus an attractive special "Select 3-Speed Service" logo, which also includes the logo of then-partner KLM. Since March 2008 it has flown in typical NWA colors. Being retired in December 2009, we might see this youngest member of the former NW Cargo fleet serve with another operator in the future.

**Boeing 747-222B SF**, 673rd 747, serial number 23736, built in 1986. This former United passenger liner with N151UA registration was obtained in 2000, registered N645NW, and rebuilt as a freighter by 2001. Along with its identical sister plane N646NW, it was still bearing the original special paint job, similar to that of N643NW, when parked in November 2009.

# PIA Pakistan International

Presumably inspired by British Airways, Pakistan International Airlines decided in 2006 to make its new sand-colored paint, introduced only two years before but regarded as boring, more interesting by decorating the tail fins of their planes with motifs of traditional Pakistani Moslem patterns. There are four different designs which have been used on almost all the fleet's planes by now. Appropriately for the regions represented, the planes have been given individual names and slogans that advertise the local specialties. By April 2010, however, PIA decided on another livery modification, as the colourful patterns are being replaced by a large motif based on the country's flag, covering most of the tail fin.

**Aerospatiale ATR-42-500**, 661st ATR, built in 2007. AP-BHN was delivered to PIA in 2007 and bears the design of the Northwest Frontier province.

**Boeing 777-340 ER**, 705th 777, serial number 33780, built in 2008. AP-BID was delivered to PIA in March 2008. This plane's tail design is called "Phulkari" and comes from the Northwest Frontier province.

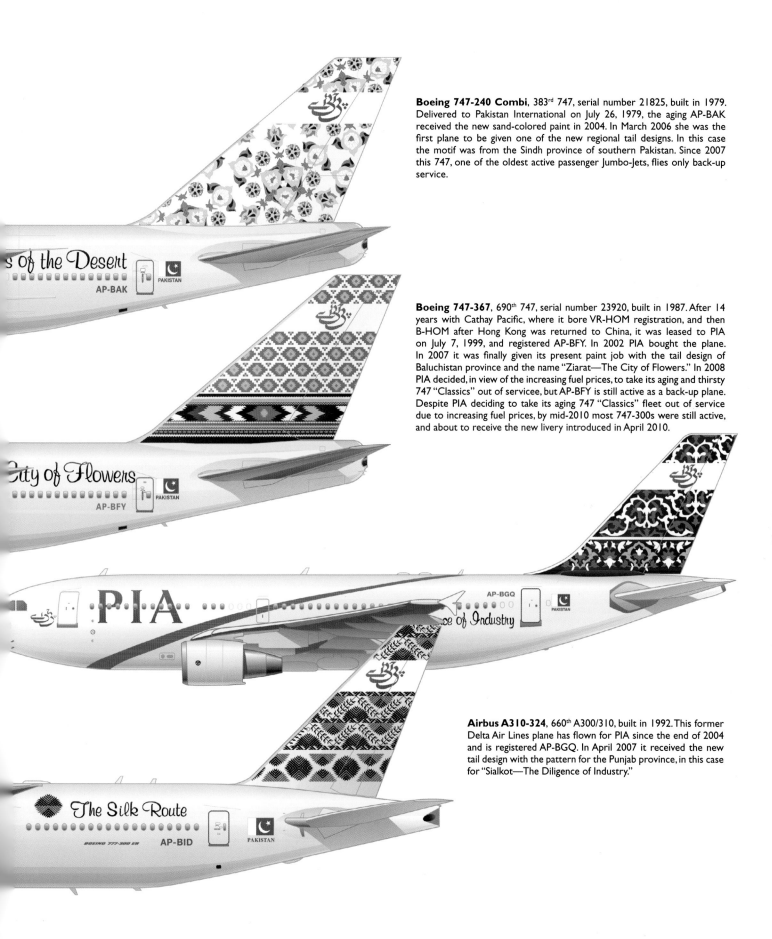

**Boeing 747-240 Combi**, 383rd 747, serial number 21825, built in 1979. Delivered to Pakistan International on July 26, 1979, the aging AP-BAK received the new sand-colored paint in 2004. In March 2006 she was the first plane to be given one of the new regional tail designs. In this case the motif was from the Sindh province of southern Pakistan. Since 2007 this 747, one of the oldest active passenger Jumbo-Jets, flies only back-up service.

**Boeing 747-367**, 690th 747, serial number 23920, built in 1987. After 14 years with Cathay Pacific, where it bore VR-HOM registration, and then B-HOM after Hong Kong was returned to China, it was leased to PIA on July 7, 1999, and registered AP-BFY. In 2002 PIA bought the plane. In 2007 it was finally given its present paint job with the tail design of Baluchistan province and the name "Ziarat—The City of Flowers." In 2008 PIA decided, in view of the increasing fuel prices, to take its aging and thirsty 747 "Classics" out of servicee, but AP-BFY is still active as a back-up plane. Despite PIA deciding to take its aging 747 "Classics" fleet out of service due to increasing fuel prices, by mid-2010 most 747-300s were still active, and about to receive the new livery introduced in April 2010.

**Airbus A310-324**, 660th A300/310, built in 1992. This former Delta Air Lines plane has flown for PIA since the end of 2004 and is registered AP-BGQ. In April 2007 it received the new tail design with the pattern for the Punjab province, in this case for "Sialkot—The Diligence of Industry."

109

# Qantas

The Australian Qantas line uses what is probably the most famous airplane with special painting, the magnificent bright red "Wunala Dreaming." With its spectacular appearance the "colorful bird" boom began for airlines all over the world. Decorated with motifs of aboriginal art and from the Balarinji Art Studio of Adelaide, it is an ideal emissary from its country like no other airplane. Strictly speaking, "Wunala Dreaming" concerns two planes. From September 1994 to the beginning of 2003 Boeing 747-438 VH-OJB bore the artistic design; since the beginning of 2003 a brand new delivery, 747-438ER, registered VH-OEJ, carries it. The planes can be distinguished only by their power plants, VH-OJB having Rolls-Royce RB211-524 engines that are included in the design, while the present-day "Wunala Dreaming" is driven by plain gray-painted General Electric CF6-80 engines.

**Boeing 747-438**, 746th 747, serial number 24373, built in 1989. VH-OJB, delivered on September 15, 1989, bore the name "City of Sydney" and was a completely normal member of the long-flight fleet until 1994. In September 1994 it became "Wunala Dreaming." Inspired by the natural colors of Australia, a team of artists at Balarinji developed probably the most spectacular paint job that an airplane has ever carried. The aboriginal culture is the oldest existing one in the world. A nucleus of their mythology consists of the "Dreamtime" legends. One of them is "Wunala Dreaming," which tells of spiritual forefathers in the form of kangaroos and their wanderings from camps to water holes. The two sides were decorated differently. Since March 2003 VH-OJB flies in standard livery again. Note, for reasons of space, the two side views are in a smaller scale than usual in this book.

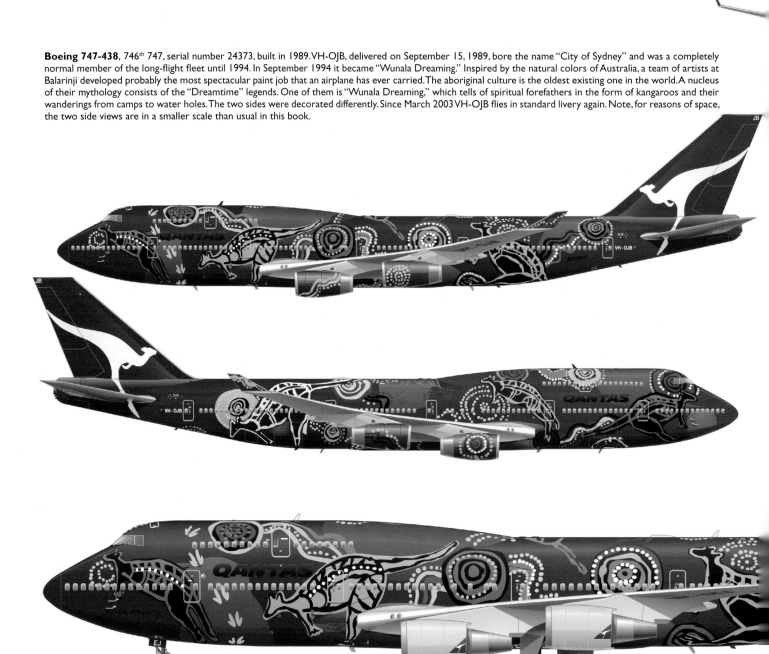

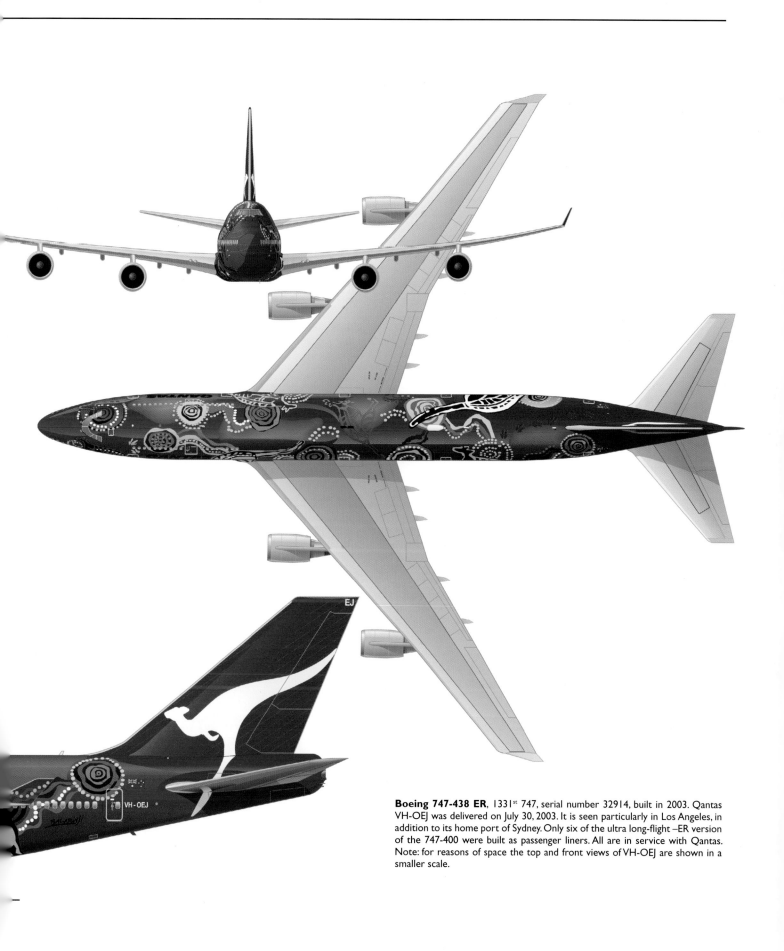

**Boeing 747-438 ER**, 1331st 747, serial number 32914, built in 2003. Qantas VH-OEJ was delivered on July 30, 2003. It is seen particularly in Los Angeles, in addition to its home port of Sydney. Only six of the ultra long-flight –ER version of the 747-400 were built as passenger liners. All are in service with Qantas. Note: for reasons of space the top and front views of VH-OEJ are shown in a smaller scale.

# Qantas

Along with "Wunala Dreaming," Qantas has two other planes decorated with aboriginal art, a Boeing 747-338 from the end of 1995 to its taking out of service in 2005 and a Boeing 737-838 since 2002.

**Boeing 737-838**, 1045th 737NG, serial number 30101, built in 2001. Delivered to Qantas on January 16, 2002, the third plane decorated by Balarinji is registered VH-VXB and is called "Yananyi Dreaming." The aboriginal artist Rene Kulitja of the Pitjantajara tribe was inspired to do this design by the desert landscape near Uluru (Ayers Rock), settled for 40,000 years. "Yananyi," in the language of the Anangu who live there, means something like going or traveling. The design on this plane, which is used only for inland transit, thus shows paths that lead to Uluru, wallaby tracks, lizards, trees, and mountains. VH-VXB was already painted by Boeing. The procedure, for which almost 500 liters of paint were needed, took six days in all. The painting also differs on the two sides, unlike the two Jumbo-Jets in aboriginal design, where both sides are identical.

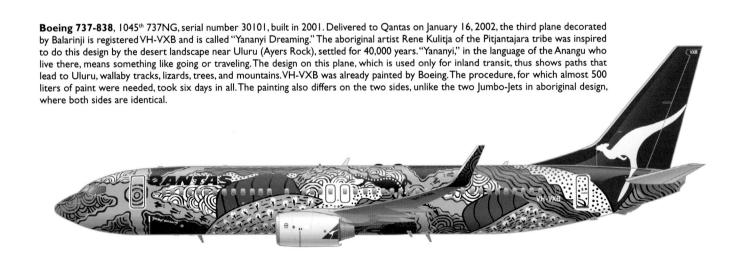

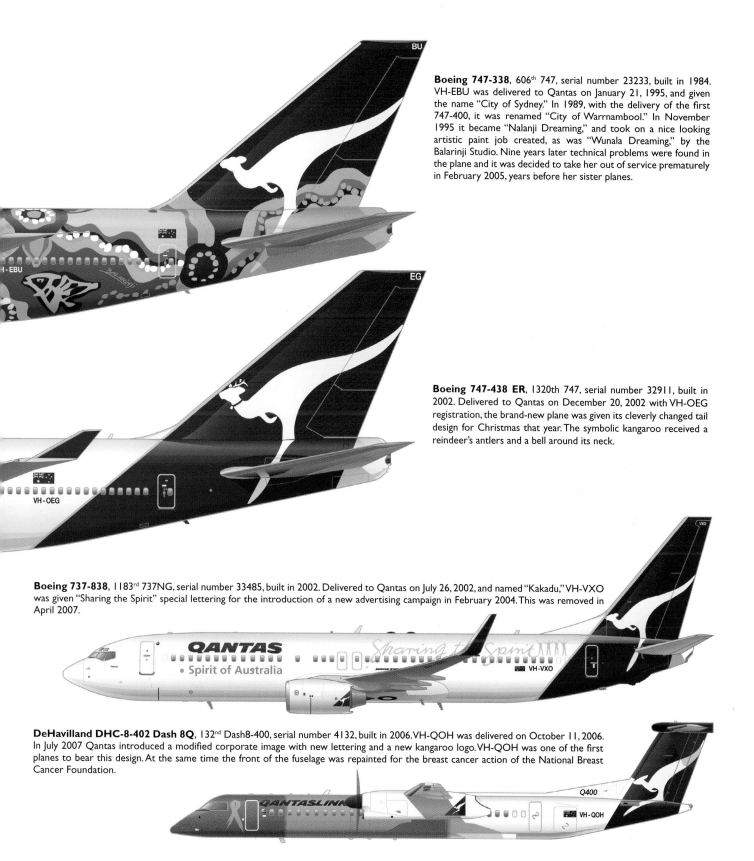

**Boeing 747-338**, 606th 747, serial number 23233, built in 1984. VH-EBU was delivered to Qantas on January 21, 1995, and given the name "City of Sydney." In 1989, with the delivery of the first 747-400, it was renamed "City of Warrnambool." In November 1995 it became "Nalanji Dreaming," and took on a nice looking artistic paint job created, as was "Wunala Dreaming," by the Balarinji Studio. Nine years later technical problems were found in the plane and it was decided to take her out of service prematurely in February 2005, years before her sister planes.

**Boeing 747-438 ER**, 1320th 747, serial number 32911, built in 2002. Delivered to Qantas on December 20, 2002 with VH-OEG registration, the brand-new plane was given its cleverly changed tail design for Christmas that year. The symbolic kangaroo received a reindeer's antlers and a bell around its neck.

**Boeing 737-838**, 1183rd 737NG, serial number 33485, built in 2002. Delivered to Qantas on July 26, 2002, and named "Kakadu," VH-VXO was given "Sharing the Spirit" special lettering for the introduction of a new advertising campaign in February 2004. This was removed in April 2007.

**DeHavilland DHC-8-402 Dash 8Q**, 132nd Dash8-400, serial number 4132, built in 2006. VH-QOH was delivered on October 11, 2006. In July 2007 Qantas introduced a modified corporate image with new lettering and a new kangaroo logo. VH-QOH was one of the first planes to bear this design. At the same time the front of the fuselage was repainted for the breast cancer action of the National Breast Cancer Foundation.

# Qantas

For Australia as a sporting nation, it is quite understandable that big sporting events are also big celebrations. In the most recent years Qantas has used a number of planes with special logos to advertise sporting events sponsored by the airline, begun with the formerly most elegant one to date, a 747 that advertised the Formula 1 Australian Grand Prix around the world.

**Boeing 747-438**, 1230th 747, serial number 25564, built 1999. VH-OJS was delivered in September 1999. Exactly ten years later, in September 2009, this plane called "Hamilton Island" received the new, well, better it should be called revised, livery of Qantas, and only one month afterwards it got huge "Qantas socceroos" stickers in the shape of a ball and a scarf in team colours to celebrate the participation of the national soccer team in the World Championship of 2010 in South Africa.

**Boeing 767-336 ER**, 293rd 767, serial number 24388, built in 1990. The Boeing, delivered to British Airways on June 23, 1990, with G-BNWF registration, was leased to Qantas on October 31, 2000, along with several sister planes and reregistered VH-ZXB. It carried the same rugby sticker on the tail as its big sister VH-OEH above. In 2006 VH-ZXB was used again to support a big sporting event. This time it bore a striking advertisement for the Australian national team "Qantas Socceroos" that took part in the 2006 world soccer championship in Germany.

**Boeing 767-338 ER**, 402nd 747, serial number 25363, built in 1991. Delivered to Qantas on November 21, 1991. Named "City of Wangaratta," VH-OGL was only another unspectacular 767 in the fleet until in 2007 it was given large labels in the form of sport scarves to promote the Qantas "Wallabies" Australian national rugby team in the Rugby World Cup. Like all special Qantas paint jobs, this short-lived design was also stylish as it was witty.

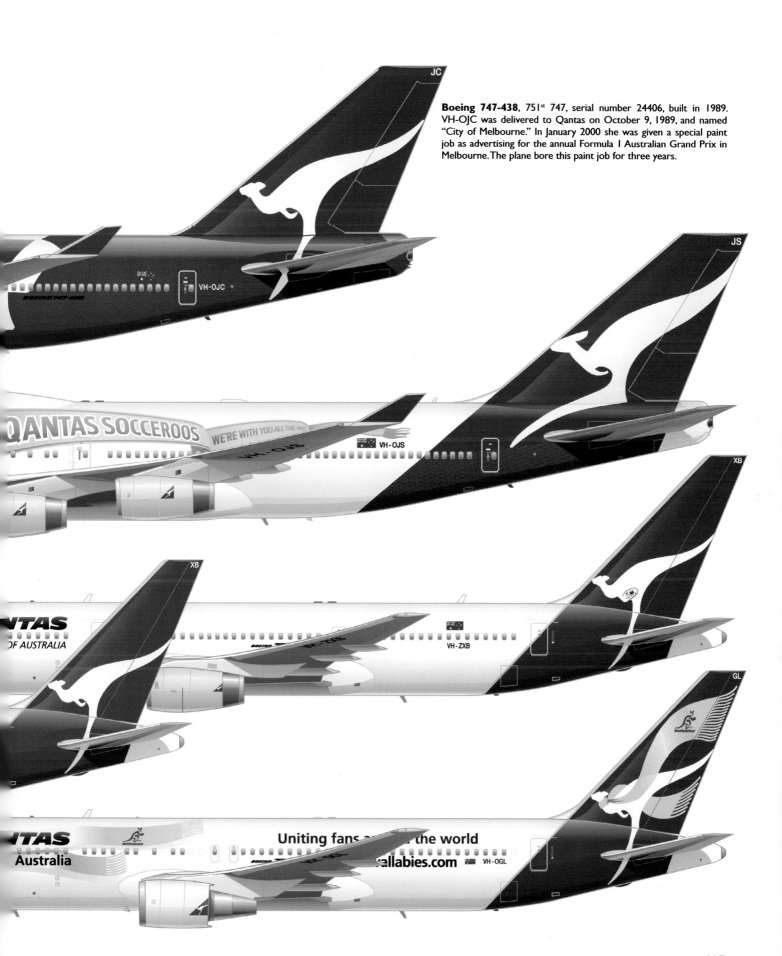

**Boeing 747-438**, 751st 747, serial number 24406, built in 1989. VH-OJC was delivered to Qantas on October 9, 1989, and named "City of Melbourne." In January 2000 she was given a special paint job as advertising for the annual Formula 1 Australian Grand Prix in Melbourne. The plane bore this paint job for three years.

# Ryanair

The low-cost carrier from Ireland put advertisements on their airplanes almost from the start. Advertisements for themselves, gibes at their competitors, and also advertising for other firms, newspapers, cars, glass, and beer. Good taste was not always involved, but advertising is like that. Ryanair has always aimed at a monoculture type, from 1994 to the beginning of the new century on secondhand 737-200s, and since then on larger, brand new 737-800s. Here is a selection of Ryanair logo jets with no pretense of completeness.

**Boeing 737-2T5**, 636th 737, serial number 22023, built in 1980, delivered to Orion Airways on February 11, 1980, with G-BGTW registration. The plane was leased by Ryanair on June 1, 1995, with EI-CKS registration. It was painted like a billboard, with huge lettering all along the side. At Christmas of 1995 the nose was adorned with a clever decoration, while in 1997 it bore special "Love Plane" stickers. In 2004, at 24 years old, it was taken out of service, and in 2005 it was scrapped.

**Boeing 737-230**, 694th 737, serial number 22115, built in 1980. Delivered to Lufthansa on December 19, 1980, D-ABFC bore the name "Würzburg." Sold to Ryanair on December 3, 1996, EI-CNT became an advertisement for the British boulevard newspapers "The Sun" (left side) and "News of the World" (right side). At the beginning of 2002 the hushkits attached by Lufthansa were removed and the plane became an advertisement for Vodafone until it was retired in October 2005. After that it served for three years with LAN Airlines with CC-CQQ registration.

**Boeing 737-230**, 745th 737, serial number 22127, built in 1981. Delivered to Lufthansa on April 16, 1981, with D-ABFW registration and the name "Wolfsburg," it went to Ryanair on July 3, 1997, where the basic Lufthansa colors with a gray underside were kept. EI-CNX bore Tipperary Crystal advertising in 1999-2000. In November 2005 it was taken out of service. Since February 16, 2006, it has flown for LAN Airlines with CC-CQS registration until 2008, and since then for Rutaca of Venezuela.

**Boeing 737-230**, 848th 737, serial number 22637, built in 1982. Condor was its first owner, the plane being delivered with D-ABHX registration on March 17, 1982. From November 1997 to October 16, 2004, it flew for Ryanair with EI-COA registration. For a short time, until the beginning of 1998, it bore a special Christmas logo. From May 26, 2005, until it was taken out of service in 2008 this plane flew for the Indonesian Adam Air as PK-KKJ.

**Boeing 737-204**, 863rd 737, serial number 22639, built in 1982. Britannia Airways put it into service on April 20, 1982, as G-BJCU, and gave it the name of the famous auto builder Sir Henry Royce. On March 17, 1994, it went to Ryanair and was registered EI-CJE. In 1997 it was given Jaguar advertising, probably the best looking special painting in the Ryanair fleet. It was taken out of service on June 2004 and rebuilt as a flight simulator.

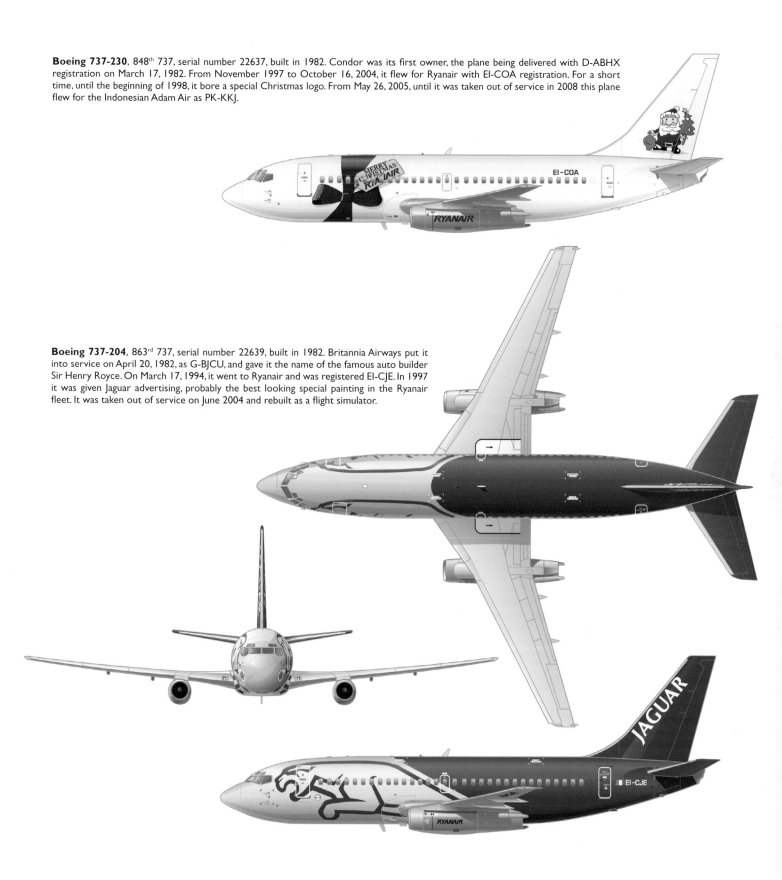

# Ryanair

Boeing 737-204, 867th 737, serial number 22640, built in 1982. This plane was also a member of the Britannia Airways fleet at first, being delivered on April 30, 1982, as G-BJCV and bearing the name of aviation pioneer Viscount Trenchard. Delivered to Ryanair on January 21, 1994, as EI-CJC, it became an advertiser for the Hertz auto rental firm five years later. Retired in November 2004, it spent a shadow life for two years until it found a buyer, Star Peru, on June 22, 2006, and was registered OB-1839-P.

Boeing 737-2E7, 917th 737, serial number 22875, built in 1982. Its first user was Arkia of Israel, who received it on March 2, 1983, with 4X-BAB registration. Sold to Ryanair on July 8, 1994, the plane was registered EI-CJI and bore a special Santa Claus logo on its nose at Christmas 1994. In 1997 London-Stockholm labels were attached. It was taken out of service in January 2005 and has been in Birmingham since then.

Boeing 737-204, 946th 737, serial number 22966, built in 1983. G-BKHE was sold to Britannia Airways on February 25, 1983; Ryanair leased it in 1994 and registered it EI-CJD. At Christmas 1995 it was given a Santa Claus nose like that of its sister plane EI-CJI a year before. In 1996 it was made into an advertisement for the London-Glasgow service with a Scottish scarf. Since then it has carried "Eircell" advertising, was taken out of service on November 2003, and is now used as a trainer at the Dublin airport.

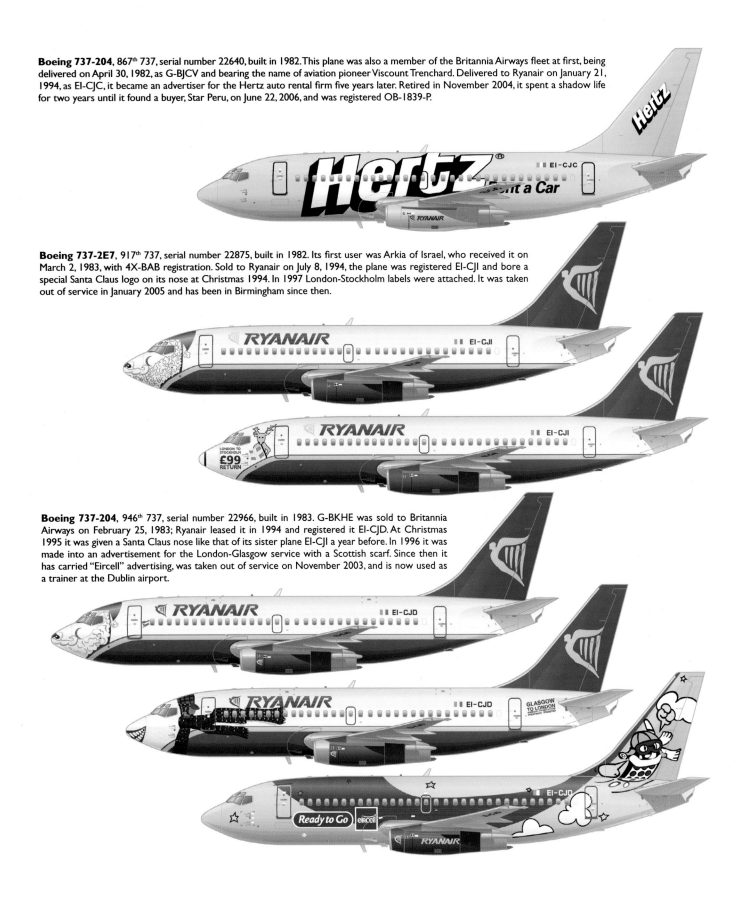

**Boeing 737-8AS**, 307th Next Generation 737, serial number 29918, built in 1999. Delivered on June 28, 1999, EI-CSC was painted at the beginning of 2005 as an advertisement for the Cable & Wireless telecommunications firm. In November 2007 it was sold and has flown since then for Varig with PR-VBC registration, and since 2009 for GOL of Brazil.

**Boeing 737-8AS**, 1178th 737NG, serial number 32780, built in 2002. EI-CSZ, delivered in the old livery on July 15, 2002, bore anti-Alitalia advertising until mid-2008. Meanwhile it was fitted with winglets at the end of 2006. By the end of 2010 the aircraft was handed over to Russian Atlant-Soyuz Airlines.

**Boeing 737-8AS**, 1252nd 737NG, serial number 33545, built in 2002. EI-DAE has flown for Ryanair since December 9, 2002. In 2004 it received "Girona-Catalunya" labels; in 2005 it also had a rugby motif applied to its nose as advertising for the southern Irish province of Munster. By the spring of 2010 it was repainted in the new livery and the adverts were removed.

**Boeing 747-8AS**, 1576th 737NG, serial number 33806, built in 2004, and in 2010 still bears the Boeing Dreamliner logo. EI-DCL was delivered on October 2, 2004.

# Singapore Airlines

This airline, doubtless ranking among the world's best, has been very restrained about special paintings. After two planes (a Boeing 747-400 and a 777-200) were given a special design with golden ribbons for the line's 50th anniversary in 1997, two Boeing 747-400s were given an attractive and very eye-catching paint job in 1999 to advertise comfortable new seats.

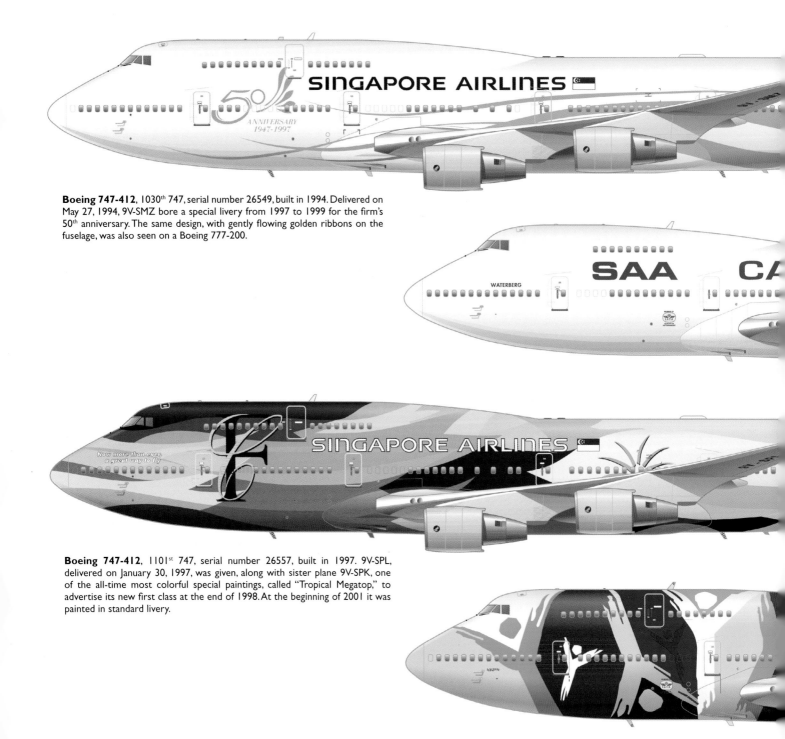

**Boeing 747-412**, 1030th 747, serial number 26549, built in 1994. Delivered on May 27, 1994, 9V-SMZ bore a special livery from 1997 to 1999 for the firm's 50th anniversary. The same design, with gently flowing golden ribbons on the fuselage, was also seen on a Boeing 777-200.

**Boeing 747-412**, 1101st 747, serial number 26557, built in 1997. 9V-SPL, delivered on January 30, 1997, was given, along with sister plane 9V-SPK, one of the all-time most colorful special paintings, called "Tropical Megatop," to advertise its new first class at the end of 1998. At the beginning of 2001 it was painted in standard livery.

# South African Airways

The South African flag carrier has scarcely taken a chance to advertise itself or its homeland with a strikingly painted airplane to date. The only one worth noting is the Boeing 747 "Ndizani," which is one of the most attractively painted planes that ever flew.

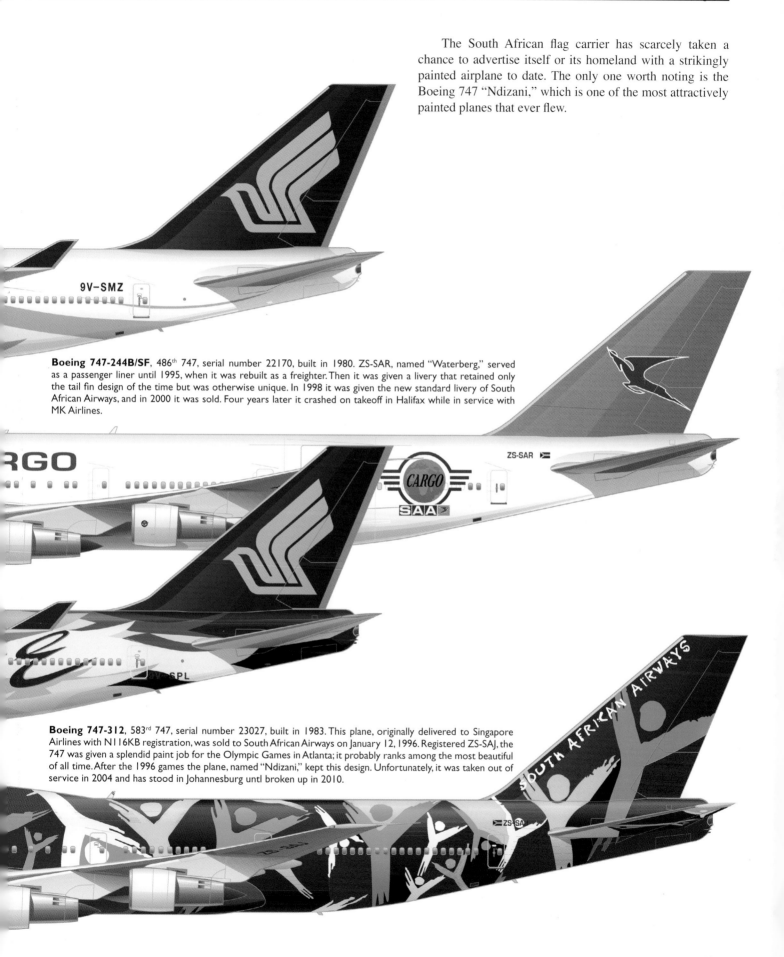

**Boeing 747-244B/SF**, 486th 747, serial number 22170, built in 1980. ZS-SAR, named "Waterberg," served as a passenger liner until 1995, when it was rebuilt as a freighter. Then it was given a livery that retained only the tail fin design of the time but was otherwise unique. In 1998 it was given the new standard livery of South African Airways, and in 2000 it was sold. Four years later it crashed on takeoff in Halifax while in service with MK Airlines.

**Boeing 747-312**, 583rd 747, serial number 23027, built in 1983. This plane, originally delivered to Singapore Airlines with N116KB registration, was sold to South African Airways on January 12, 1996. Registered ZS-SAJ, the 747 was given a splendid paint job for the Olympic Games in Atlanta; it probably ranks among the most beautiful of all time. After the 1996 games the plane, named "Ndizani," kept this design. Unfortunately, it was taken out of service in 2004 and has stood in Johannesburg untl broken up in 2010.

# TAM

After the failure of the venerable flag carrier Varig in 2006, its competitor TAM was Brazil's only important international airline. For years this line, active only regionally until the late 1990s, has had a weakness for special paintings.

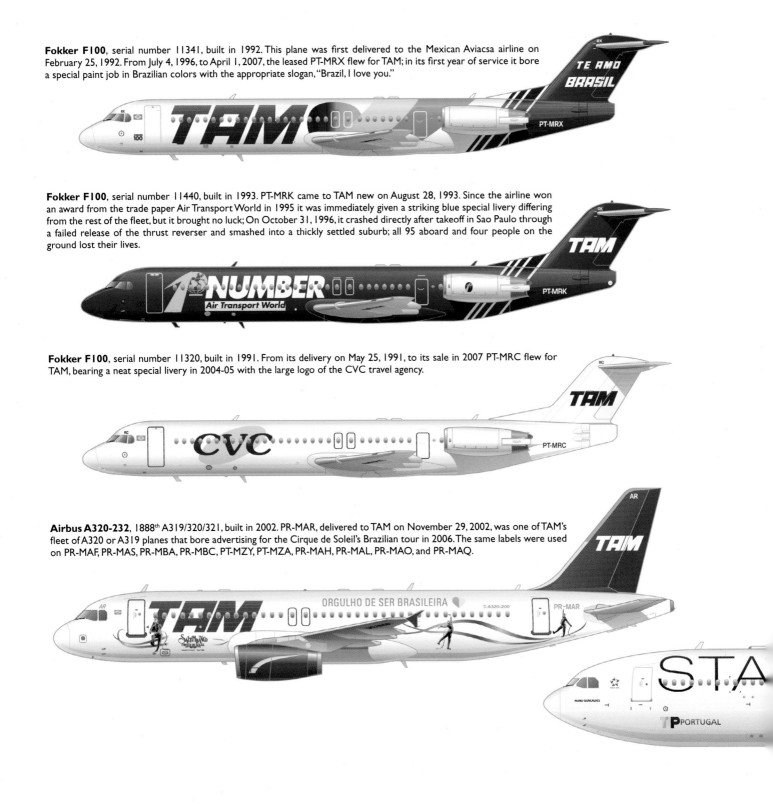

**Fokker F100**, serial number 11341, built in 1992. This plane was first delivered to the Mexican Aviacsa airline on February 25, 1992. From July 4, 1996, to April 1, 2007, the leased PT-MRX flew for TAM; in its first year of service it bore a special paint job in Brazilian colors with the appropriate slogan, "Brazil, I love you."

**Fokker F100**, serial number 11440, built in 1993. PT-MRK came to TAM new on August 28, 1993. Since the airline won an award from the trade paper Air Transport World in 1995 it was immediately given a striking blue special livery differing from the rest of the fleet, but it brought no luck; On October 31, 1996, it crashed directly after takeoff in Sao Paulo through a failed release of the thrust reverser and smashed into a thickly settled suburb; all 95 aboard and four people on the ground lost their lives.

**Fokker F100**, serial number 11320, built in 1991. From its delivery on May 25, 1991, to its sale in 2007 PT-MRC flew for TAM, bearing a neat special livery in 2004-05 with the large logo of the CVC travel agency.

**Airbus A320-232**, 1888th A319/320/321, built in 2002. PR-MAR, delivered to TAM on November 29, 2002, was one of TAM's fleet of A320 or A319 planes that bore advertising for the Cirque de Soleil's Brazilian tour in 2006. The same labels were used on PR-MAF, PR-MAS, PR-MBA, PR-MBC, PT-MZY, PT-MZA, PR-MAH, PR-MAL, PR-MAO, and PR-MAQ.

Portugal's national airline painted two of its Boeing 737s with elaborate special patterns in 1997, one as an advertisement for the Algarve vacation region, the other to promote the Expo taking place in Lisbon in 1998. Since the end of the nineties the 737s have been replaced by A320-series Airbus planes, one of which became the logo jet for the now-defunct Airline Alliance Qualiflyer in 2000-2001. In 2004 the European soccer championship was held in Portugal, and TAP gave one A319 a special paint job with photo murals, which actually does more to promote the country in general than the soccer championship. In 2006 TAP finally bought several secondhand A330s, one of which was chosen as the Star Alliance logo plane.

**Boeing 737-382**, 1699th 737, serial number 24366, built in 1989. CS-TIC, belonging to ILFC, came to TAP April 6, 1989. The plane, named "Algarve," was leased for exactly ten years. At the end of its time in Portugal it was used briefly as advertising for the Algarve, the country's most important vacation area. After several stops along the way it now flies for the Bolivian Aerosur line as CP-2640.

**Airbus A319-111**, 906th A319/A320/A321, built in 1998. CS-TTG was turned over to TAP on November 5, 1998, and named "Humberto Delgado" after the airline's founder. In 2000-2001 it bore the logo of the Qualiflyer Group, which ceased to exist after Swissair failed at the end of 2001. Since the end of 2006 this plane bears the markings for the alliance's tenth anniversary.

**Airbus A330-323**, 181st A33/340, built in 1997. After this plane had spent two years as a member of the Airbus test fleet, and had had its engine types changed completely twice, it was finally delivered to Austrian Airlines on January 17, 2000, with OE-LAO registration. Since then it flew with various Star Alliance logos. This remained so after it was sold to TAP in June 2006. The logo on the tail fin was positioned quite individually after the change of ownership. In 2007 the plane, registered CS-TOH and named "Nuno Goncalves," was given special markings for the Star Alliance's tenth anniversary.

# Thai Airways

From the end of 1999 on, Thai Airways had one of the world's loveliest and most elaborate special liveries in use. Two Boeing 747-400s flew until 2005 as "Royal Barks" for "Amazing Thailand," and an A330 is still doing so early in 2009. In March 2010 Boeing 747-400 HS-TGP was painted in a smart retro livery celebrating Thai Airways' 50th anniversary. In 2004 Thai founded the low-cost branch "Nok," in which colorful paint jobs that look like birds and advertising logos are the standard program. This little airline flies exclusively Boeing 737-400s, beginning with three transferred from the mother airline, to which several from various sources were added later.

**Boeing 737-4D7**, 2330th 737, serial number 26612, built in 1992. Delivered on July 22, 1992, HS-TDE, named "Surin," flew for Thai Airways until it was transferred to the newly founded Nok Air in October 2004. A year later it was given advertising labels for the TOT telecommunications firm; they were removed in 2007.

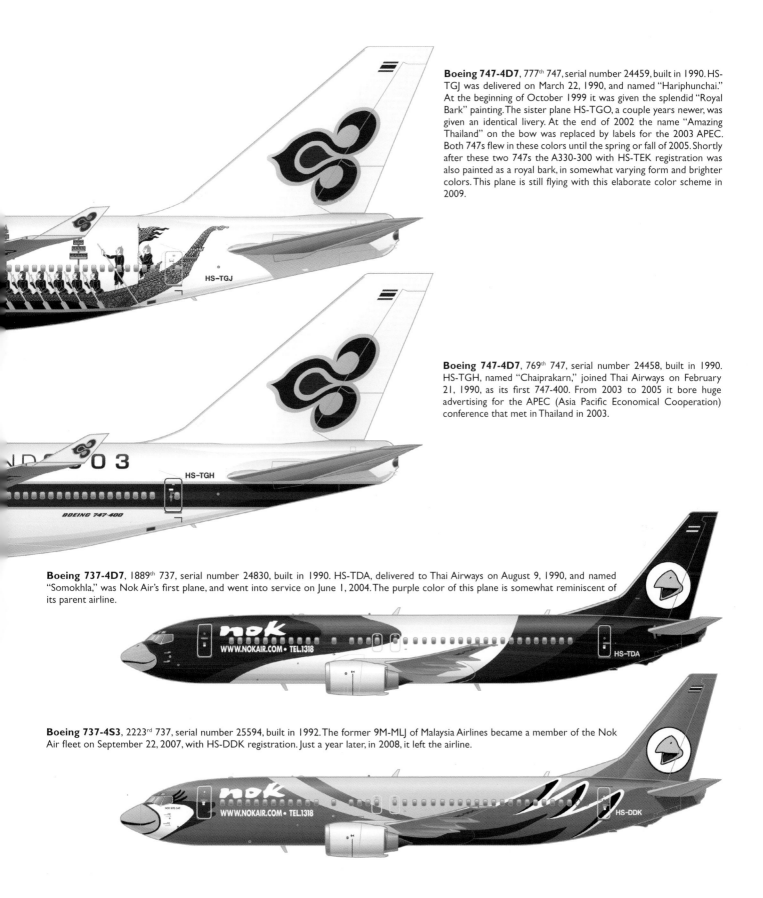

**Boeing 747-4D7**, 777th 747, serial number 24459, built in 1990. HS-TGJ was delivered on March 22, 1990, and named "Hariphunchai." At the beginning of October 1999 it was given the splendid "Royal Bark" painting. The sister plane HS-TGO, a couple years newer, was given an identical livery. At the end of 2002 the name "Amazing Thailand" on the bow was replaced by labels for the 2003 APEC. Both 747s flew in these colors until the spring or fall of 2005. Shortly after these two 747s the A330-300 with HS-TEK registration was also painted as a royal bark, in somewhat varying form and brighter colors. This plane is still flying with this elaborate color scheme in 2009.

HS-TGJ

**Boeing 747-4D7**, 769th 747, serial number 24458, built in 1990. HS-TGH, named "Chaiprakarn," joined Thai Airways on February 21, 1990, as its first 747-400. From 2003 to 2005 it bore huge advertising for the APEC (Asia Pacific Economical Cooperation) conference that met in Thailand in 2003.

HS-TGH

BOEING 747-400

**Boeing 737-4D7**, 1889th 737, serial number 24830, built in 1990. HS-TDA, delivered to Thai Airways on August 9, 1990, and named "Somokhla," was Nok Air's first plane, and went into service on June 1, 2004. The purple color of this plane is somewhat reminiscent of its parent airline.

HS-TDA

**Boeing 737-4S3**, 2223rd 737, serial number 25594, built in 1992. The former 9M-MLJ of Malaysia Airlines became a member of the Nok Air fleet on September 22, 2007, with HS-DDK registration. Just a year later, in 2008, it left the airline.

HS-DDK

# US Airways

Of the great airlines of the United States, US Airways has the greatest number of specially painted airplanes in its fleet. Yet it was the last to take up this marketing idea. In 2004 two planes had their fuselage color removed to make the advertising for the website more striking. In 2005 US Airways merged with America West Airlines, the last purchase in a long series of airlines that had been swallowed up by US Airways since the eighties. Since there were several well-known names among those vanished airlines, it was decided in 2006 to paint one A319 each in the colors of those historic firms. PSA (Pacific Southwest Airlines), Piedmont Airlines, Allegheny Airlines, and finally America West can be cited. In addition, the tradition of painting individual planes in the colors of American states and large sport teams was adopted from America West.

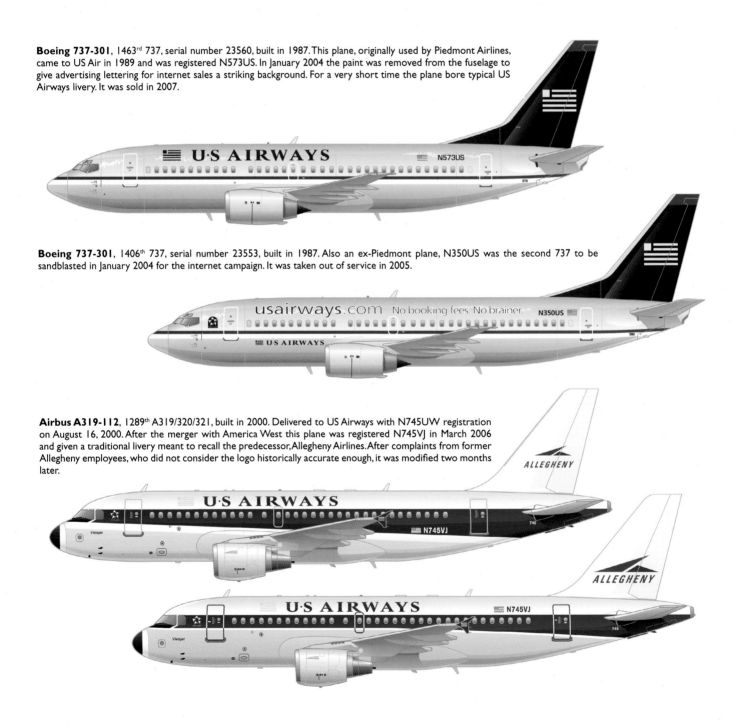

**Boeing 737-301**, 1463rd 737, serial number 23560, built in 1987. This plane, originally used by Piedmont Airlines, came to US Air in 1989 and was registered N573US. In January 2004 the paint was removed from the fuselage to give advertising lettering for internet sales a striking background. For a very short time the plane bore typical US Airways livery. It was sold in 2007.

**Boeing 737-301**, 1406th 737, serial number 23553, built in 1987. Also an ex-Piedmont plane, N350US was the second 737 to be sandblasted in January 2004 for the internet campaign. It was taken out of service in 2005.

**Airbus A319-112**, 1289th A319/320/321, built in 2000. Delivered to US Airways with N745UW registration on August 16, 2000. After the merger with America West this plane was registered N745VJ in March 2006 and given a traditional livery meant to recall the predecessor, Allegheny Airlines. After complaints from former Allegheny employees, who did not consider the logo historically accurate enough, it was modified two months later.

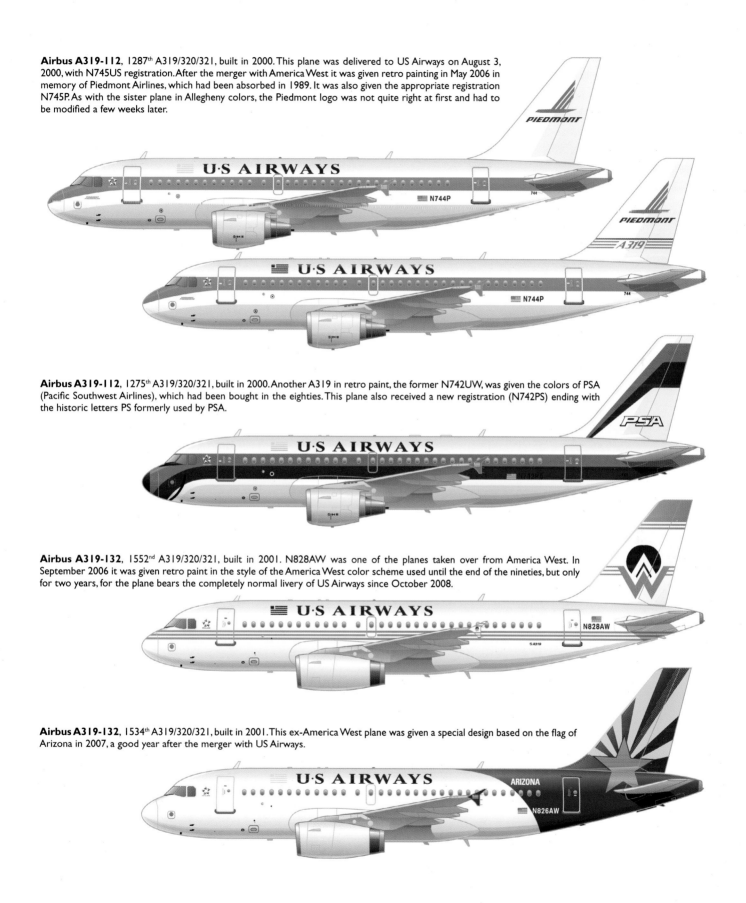

**Airbus A319-112**, 1287th A319/320/321, built in 2000. This plane was delivered to US Airways on August 3, 2000, with N745US registration. After the merger with America West it was given retro painting in May 2006 in memory of Piedmont Airlines, which had been absorbed in 1989. It was also given the appropriate registration N745P. As with the sister plane in Allegheny colors, the Piedmont logo was not quite right at first and had to be modified a few weeks later.

**Airbus A319-112**, 1275th A319/320/321, built in 2000. Another A319 in retro paint, the former N742UW, was given the colors of PSA (Pacific Southwest Airlines), which had been bought in the eighties. This plane also received a new registration (N742PS) ending with the historic letters PS formerly used by PSA.

**Airbus A319-132**, 1552nd A319/320/321, built in 2001. N828AW was one of the planes taken over from America West. In September 2006 it was given retro paint in the style of the America West color scheme used until the end of the nineties, but only for two years, for the plane bears the completely normal livery of US Airways since October 2008.

**Airbus A319-132**, 1534th A319/320/321, built in 2001. This ex-America West plane was given a special design based on the flag of Arizona in 2007, a good year after the merger with US Airways.

# Varig

No other nation is as crazy about soccer as the Brazilians. One can see that from their airplanes, and naturally their pilots. Varig, a longtime flag carrier, has decorated more than ten planes with soccer motifs ever since the beginning of the nineties, when one DC 10 began the trend. In particular two planes, a long-flight type and a 737, bore the designs of each of the four-year world championships. In addition several other jets, mainly Boeing 737s, have borne the most varied advertising or anniversary logos.

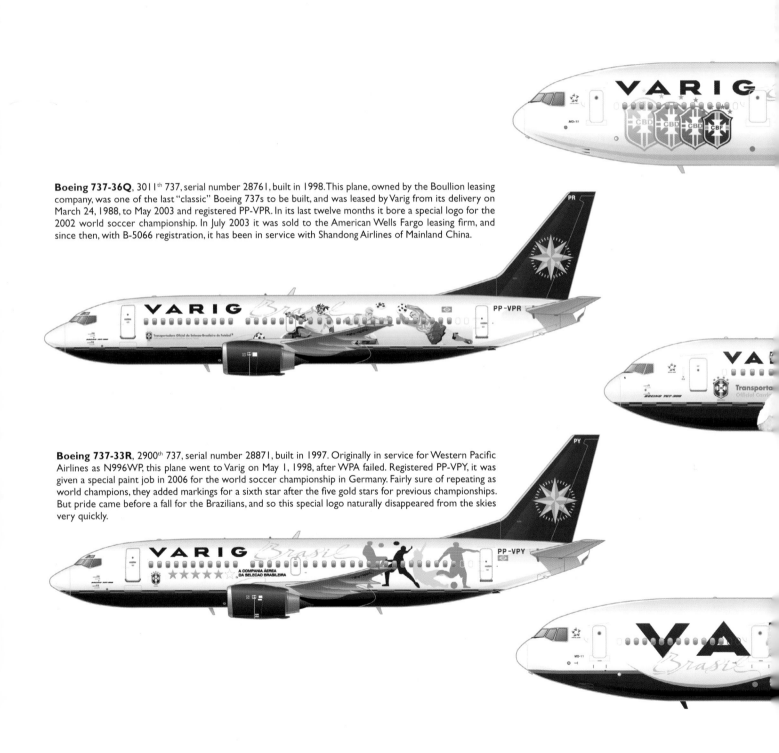

**Boeing 737-36Q**, 3011th 737, serial number 28761, built in 1998. This plane, owned by the Boullion leasing company, was one of the last "classic" Boeing 737s to be built, and was leased by Varig from its delivery on March 24, 1988, to May 2003 and registered PP-VPR. In its last twelve months it bore a special logo for the 2002 world soccer championship. In July 2003 it was sold to the American Wells Fargo leasing firm, and since then, with B-5066 registration, it has been in service with Shandong Airlines of Mainland China.

**Boeing 737-33R**, 2900th 737, serial number 28871, built in 1997. Originally in service for Western Pacific Airlines as N996WP, this plane went to Varig on May 1, 1998, after WPA failed. Registered PP-VPY, it was given a special paint job in 2006 for the world soccer championship in Germany. Fairly sure of repeating as world champions, they added markings for a sixth star after the five gold stars for previous championships. But pride came before a fall for the Brazilians, and so this special logo naturally disappeared from the skies very quickly.

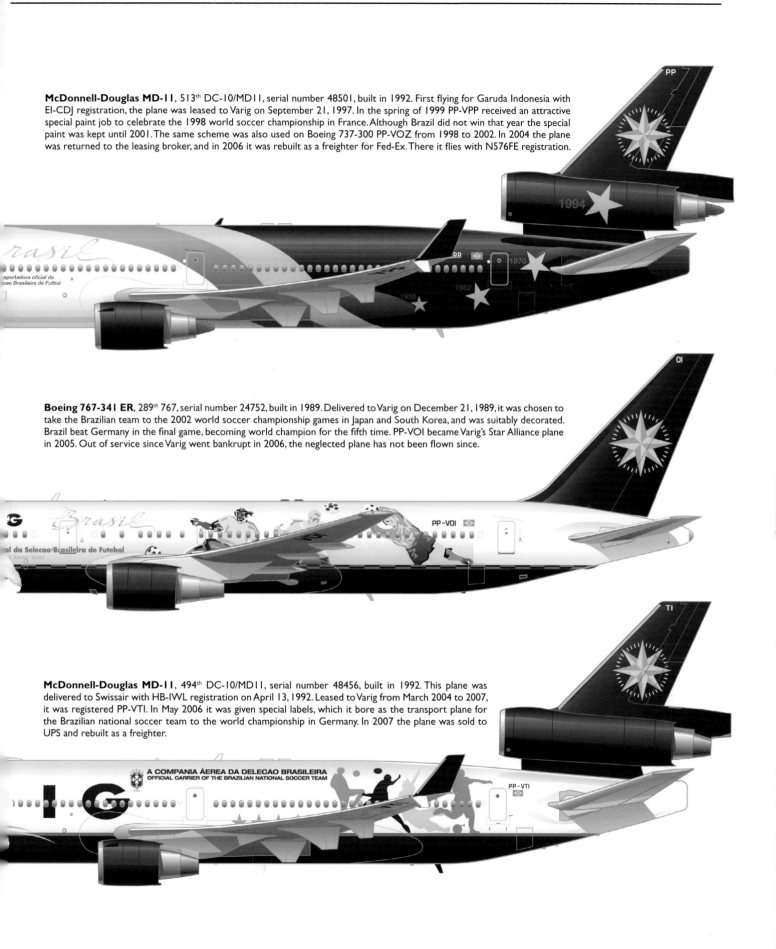

**McDonnell-Douglas MD-11**, 513th DC-10/MD11, serial number 48501, built in 1992. First flying for Garuda Indonesia with EI-CDJ registration, the plane was leased to Varig on September 21, 1997. In the spring of 1999 PP-VPP received an attractive special paint job to celebrate the 1998 world soccer championship in France. Although Brazil did not win that year the special paint was kept until 2001. The same scheme was also used on Boeing 737-300 PP-VOZ from 1998 to 2002. In 2004 the plane was returned to the leasing broker, and in 2006 it was rebuilt as a freighter for Fed-Ex. There it flies with N576FE registration.

**Boeing 767-341 ER**, 289th 767, serial number 24752, built in 1989. Delivered to Varig on December 21, 1989, it was chosen to take the Brazilian team to the 2002 world soccer championship games in Japan and South Korea, and was suitably decorated. Brazil beat Germany in the final game, becoming world champion for the fifth time. PP-VOI became Varig's Star Alliance plane in 2005. Out of service since Varig went bankrupt in 2006, the neglected plane has not been flown since.

**McDonnell-Douglas MD-11**, 494th DC-10/MD11, serial number 48456, built in 1992. This plane was delivered to Swissair with HB-IWL registration on April 13, 1992. Leased to Varig from March 2004 to 2007, it was registered PP-VTI. In May 2006 it was given special labels, which it bore as the transport plane for the Brazilian national soccer team to the world championship in Germany. In 2007 the plane was sold to UPS and rebuilt as a freighter.

# Varig

**Boeing 747-341 Combi**, 629th 747, serial number 23395, built in 1985. Delivered on 19 December, PP-VNI was chosen to represent Varig as one of the first members of the Star Alliance, which became the largest and most successful worldwide group of airlines. For a few days in April 1997 the left side of the plane was painted to represent the six founding members. The right side was painted in the colors of the new Varig livery introduced at the same time. The Boeing flew three more years for Varig; after that it was then sold, rebuilt as a freighter, and sold to Atlas Air. When we went to press in 2010 it was still in service there as N355MC.

**Boeing 737-7Q8**, 369th Next Generation 737, serial number 28224, built in 1999. This plane, owned by the largest leasing firm, ILFC, flew as LV-PIG for the Argentine LAPA until the line went bankrupt in 2002. In August 2002 it was rented by the Varig branch of Rio Sul and transferred to Varig itself at the end of 2004. There it was given a simple special livery as part of a new advertising campaign. It bore this special title until Varig collapsed in May 2006. When Varig was bought months later by the Brazilian GOL line this plane passed to the new owners, who registered it as PR-GIK.

**Boeing 767-341ER**, 314th 777, serial number 24843, built in 1990. PP-VOK was delivered on June 27, 1990, and flew in the old Varig livery until the beginning of 2000, when it was chosen to be Varig's representative for Brazil's 500th anniversary. Until it was sold in 2005 it bore this special livery, with three stripes in the country's colors wrapped around the fuselage. Since July 2005 it flies as SP-LPE for the Polish LOT line, also in special colors, and has carried the black and white Star Alliance logo.

**Boeing 777-2Q8ER**, 373rd 777, serial number 28692, built in 2001. Leased to Varig by the ILFC leasing firm on November 19, 2001, as its second Triple Seven and registered as PP-VRB, it and its sister plane PP-VRA were fitted in 2002 with large labels for the 75th anniversary of the airline. The original Varig unfortunately did not get much older, as it had to declare bankruptcy in June 2006. In the same year it was reactivated in a smaller scale under new ownership. PP-VRB was retired in mid-2007 and then leased to Aeromexico as N776AM.

**Boeing 737-3S3**, 3061st 737, serial number 29245, built in 1998. PP-VPZ was delivered factory-new to Varig on September 17, 1998. In 2002 and 2003 the plane bore large labels for the firm's 75th anniversary. At the end of 2003 new special labels were affixed to PP-VPZ, this time with new year wishes. Its sister plane PP-VPX received similar but different labels to greet the year 2004. When Varig collapsed in 2006, PP-VPZ went on to Norwegian Air Shuttle.

# Virgin Atlantic

The charismatic Briton Richard (now Sir Richard) Branson, the prototype of the entrepreneur successful in many realms, founded the Virgin Atlantic airline in 1984 as an economical alternative to the established international lines. To this day it has found success in the marketplace and had always remained a bit avant-garde. Remarkably, though, there are scarcely any liveries that can truly be called special on the exclusively four-engine planes of the fleet. Additionally to the three aircraft shown here Virgin introduced a special livery in May 2010, which is a promotion jet for the well known wizard boy Harry Potter.

**Boeing 747-287B**, 274th 747, serial number 21189, built in 1976. The former LV-LZD, the first 747 of Aerolineas Argentinas, also became the first plane of the newly founded Virgin Atlantic and thus the basis of a success story. Very much in the spirit of the marketing jokes of its ebullient owner Richard Branson, the "Maiden Voyager" was given a clever tail fin design showing a sign painter falling from a scaffold; this detail caused much annoyance and was even taken seriously, so it was removed in 1987. Shortly before that the cockpit had been fitted with a huge pair of sunglasses for a short time. In 2001 the plane was sold to the Nigerian Kabo Air line, where it was still active until 2008.

**Boeing 747-4Q8**, 1043rd 747, serial number 26326, built in 1994. Delivered on October 1, 1994, and named "Tubular Belle" after an old Mark Oldfield hit, G-VHOT gained a chic new silver coat in 2000. In 2003 the Flying Lady had a silhouette in the colors of the Union Jack painted on the bow. Like many of the airline's planes it bore striking slogans at the rear, here advertising the advantages of four-engine planes.

**Boeing 747-4Q8**, 1028th 747, serial number 24958, built in 1994. G-VFAB belonged to the ILFC leasing firm and was transferred to Great Britain on April 28, 1994. In March 2005 it received a special paint job for the line's 21st anniversary, with a large Flying Lady and the name "Birthday Girl." An aerial balloon label was removed just a few months later, but the special paint job shown here has been kept.

# Star Alliance

In May 1997 the "Star Alliance" airline union was founded, with Air Canada, Lufthansa, SAS, Thai Airways, and United Airlines as members. These firms each painted one long-flight plane of their fleets in the Alliance livery. This first color scheme was very eye-catching, having the design of each founding member on one-sixth of the fuselage length, along with that of Varig, which had joined the Alliance shortly after it was founded. The tail fin bore the Alliance logo on a black background. Since the Star Alliance developed very quickly and included more and more members this look could not be maintained for long. In 1999 a scheme was introduced in which the logos of the members were added in colorful squares, but this design did not last long either.

Airbus A340-211, eighth A330/340, built in 1993. D-AIBA came to Lufthansa on January 29, 1994. The short A340 was named "Nürnberg" and flew in Star Alliance colors from 1997 on. At the beginning of 2003 Lufthansa sold its small A340-200 fleet to South African Airways. D-AIBA made its last flight for the crane on January 13, 2003.

Embraer ERJ-145EP, 454th ERJ135/145, built in 2001. Turned over to BMI (British Midland) on June 22, 2001, with G-RJXI registration, the regional jet still bears the interim Star Alliance livery that has been out of date for almost a decade by 2010.

Airbus A330-223, 181st A330/340, built in 1997. OE-LAO was delivered to Austrian Airlines on January 17, 2000, and named "Grossglockner" after Austria's highest mountain. The plane, which was formerly used as a test prototype by Airbus for more than two years, was painted with the interim Star Alliance livery when delivered to AUA; this was kept for two years. After that it bore the new Alliance livery for four years, though not with the white tail fin called for by the corporate image, before it was passed on to TAP Air Portugal. There it flies with CS-TOH registration.

**Boeing 767-322 ER**, 460th 767, serial number 25391, built in 1992. N635UA of United Airlines left the Seattle factory on October 27, 1992. From 1998 on it bore the first Star Alliance livery shown here, taking on the present-day look in 2004. It can be seen in this form on the next pages.

**Boeing 767-241 ER**, 181st 767, serial number 23806, built in 1987. PP-VNS was delivered on August 5, 1987. From 1997 to 2001 it was Varig's Star Alliance jet. It was taken out of service in 2003 and spent two sad years in the desert. In 2005 it was reactivated for Bellview Airlines of Nigeria. Under 5N-BGH it flew until being retired in 2009 mainly on the Lagos-London route.

# Star Alliance

New members compelled the Star Alliance to change the look of planes flying in Alliance livery yet again in 2001. Since then there are no more colorful birds but the simple, colorless, and very restrained paint job, with a white fuselage and black tail fin that was introduced. The lettering stretches over the entire length of the fuselage, and the Alliance's eponymous star glitters on the fin. The logo of the applicable airline is on the front part of the fuselage under the Star Alliance lettering, and the engines retain the airline's colors. The design has proved to be very practical for leased planes. A constantly growing number of planes now bears this simply applied paint, while Singapore Airlines in particular handles the corporate image a bit more loosely.

**McDonnell Douglas MD-11**, 498th DC10/MD11, serial number 48457, built in 1992. This plane originally flew with HB-IWM registration for Swissair. From 2004 to 2006 it was leased to Varig and was registered PP-VTH. For the fairly short leasing period this plane was chosen as the Star Alliance logo jet. In 2006 it was sold to UPS and, like the greater part of the MD-11s, which have no longer been built since 2000, was rebuilt as a freighter.

**Boeing 777-312**, 244th 777, serial number 28531, built in 1999. 9V-SYE of Singapore Airlines was put into service on September 24, 1999. It is an example of many airlines' light touch with corporate identity. In July 2004 it was given a not exactly specified Star Alliance livery. At the end of 2007, in the process of modification of Singapore Airlines' CI, the "Kris" bird emblem on the tail fin was enlarged.

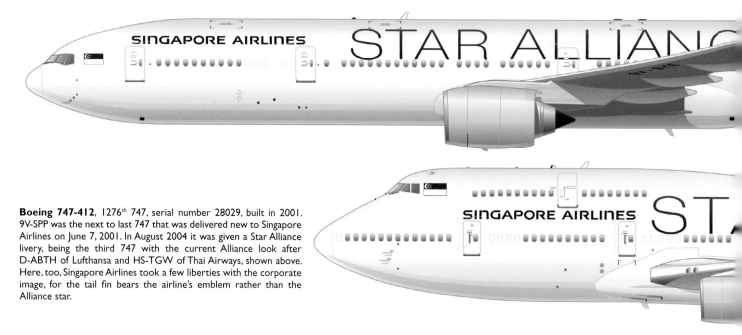

**Boeing 747-412**, 1276th 747, serial number 28029, built in 2001. 9V-SPP was the next to last 747 that was delivered new to Singapore Airlines on June 7, 2001. In August 2004 it was given a Star Alliance livery, being the third 747 with the current Alliance look after D-ABTH of Lufthansa and HS-TGW of Thai Airways, shown above. Here, too, Singapore Airlines took a few liberties with the corporate image, for the tail fin bears the airline's emblem rather than the Alliance star.

**Boeing 747-4D7**, 1111th 747, serial number 27724, built in 1997. HS-TGW left the Boeing works in Seattle on April 28, 1997. Thai Airways gave it the name "Visuthakasatriya." In June 2003 it was given Star Alliance livery.

HS-TGW

BOEING 747-400

ALLIANCE

9V-SYE

R ALLIANCE

9V-SPP

# Star Alliance

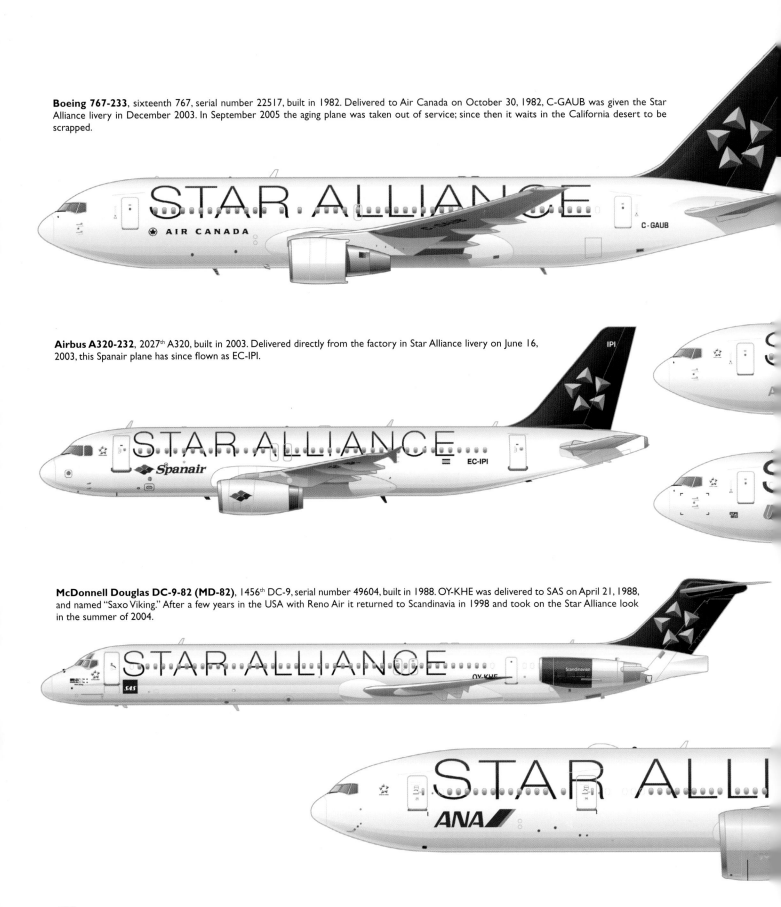

**Boeing 767-233**, sixteenth 767, serial number 22517, built in 1982. Delivered to Air Canada on October 30, 1982, C-GAUB was given the Star Alliance livery in December 2003. In September 2005 the aging plane was taken out of service; since then it waits in the California desert to be scrapped.

**Airbus A320-232**, 2027th A320, built in 2003. Delivered directly from the factory in Star Alliance livery on June 16, 2003, this Spanair plane has since flown as EC-IPI.

**McDonnell Douglas DC-9-82 (MD-82)**, 1456th DC-9, serial number 49604, built in 1988. OY-KHE was delivered to SAS on April 21, 1988, and named "Saxo Viking." After a few years in the USA with Reno Air it returned to Scandinavia in 1998 and took on the Star Alliance look in the summer of 2004.

**Boeing 737-883**, 1424th 737NG, serial number 28328, built in 2003. Delivered directly from the factory to SAS with Star Alliance livery and SE-DYT registration on December 18, 2003, the plane was named "Jarlabanke Viking," but sold to a leasing firm just a year later, though immediately leased again and given a Norse registration of LN-RRL.

**Boeing 767-38E**, 668th 767, serial number 25759, built in 1997. HL7416 left the Seattle factory on July 17, 1997, and flew six years in standard colors until, at the beginning of 1993, it became one of the first planes to take on the new Star Alliance look. In May 2007 it was given newly designed Asiana lettering and a logo for the tenth anniversary of the Star Alliance.

**Boeing 767-322 ER**, 460th 767, serial number 25391, built in 1992. N653UA has flown for United Airlines since October 27, 1992. As one can see from this plane, not all airlines stick to the really simple scheme. When it took on the present look in February 2004 United obviously did not find the right typeface.

**Boeing 777-381 ER**, 488th 777, serial number 28281, built in 2004. JA731A was given the Star Alliance livery in Seattle before being flown to Japan in November. On the overly long 777-300 the simple Star Alliance logo looks unfinished and naked.

# Star Alliance

Bombardier **CRJ700**, serial number 10100, built in 2003. Along with sister planes D-ACPQ and D-ACPT this plane, named "Berchtesgaden," forms Lufthansa Regional's Star Alliance trio.

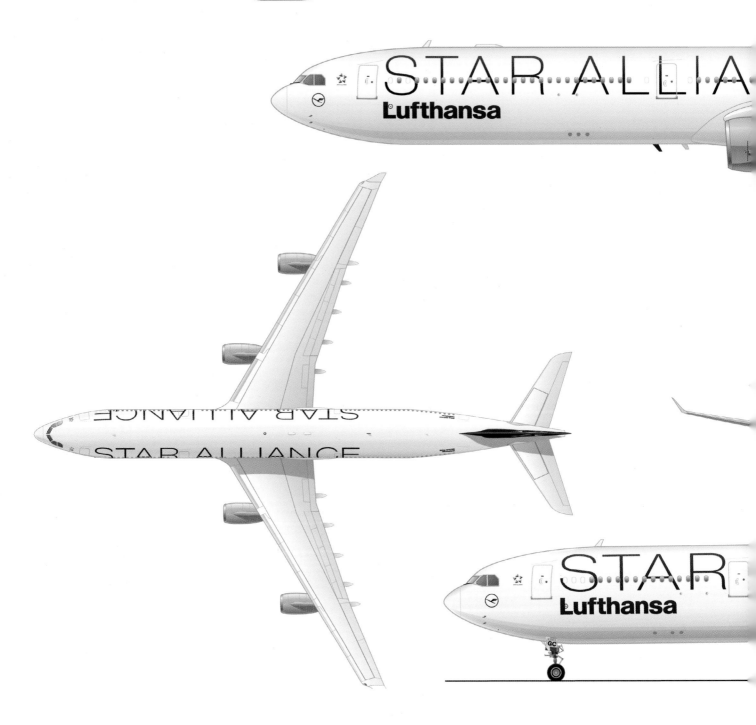

**Airbus A340-642**, 523rd A330/340, built in 2004. D-AIHC left the Toulouse factory on December 8, 2003, already in Star Alliance livery. The plane was named "Essen." In early 2009 it was repainted in standard Lufthansa colors.

**Airbus A340-311**, 27th A330/340, built in 1993. This early A340 was delivered to Lufthansa on December 2, 1993, and named "Wilhelmshaven." It was given Star Alliance livery in December 2003.

# Passenger Jets as Movie Stars

In many films, most of them about catastrophes, airplanes have played leading roles. Naturally this is only possible with imaginary painting for airline names that do not really exist. From the start, Hollywood was overwhelmed by the Boeing 747 which, thanks to its size, which overshadowed everything else for years, is perfectly suited to this genre. Since the millennium computer generated airplanes have replaced the real thing more and more, so that since then real airplanes scarcely need to be repainted for film use.

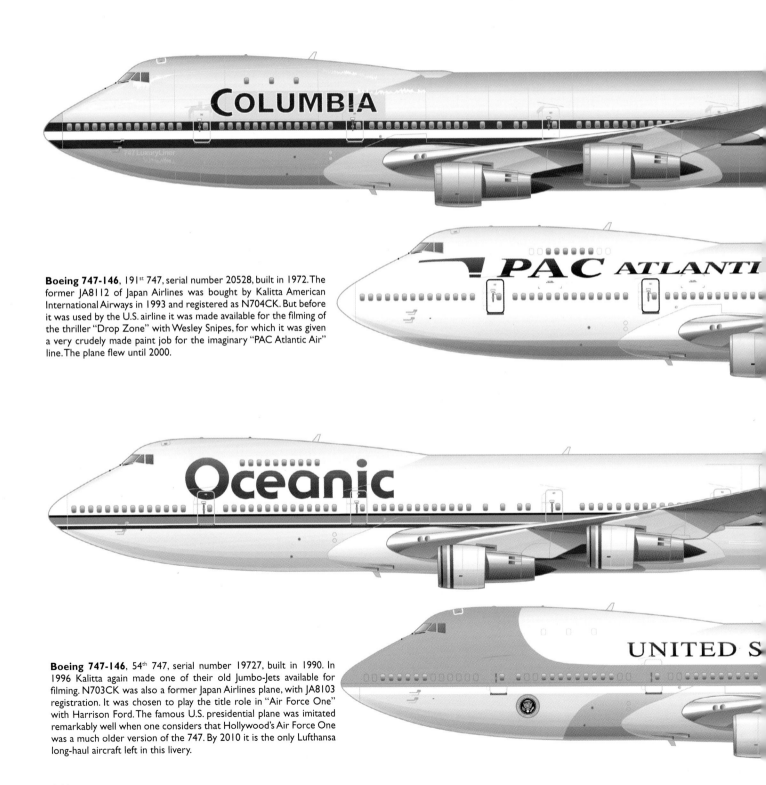

**Boeing 747-146**, 191st 747, serial number 20528, built in 1972. The former JA8112 of Japan Airlines was bought by Kalitta American International Airways in 1993 and registered as N704CK. But before it was used by the U.S. airline it was made available for the filming of the thriller "Drop Zone" with Wesley Snipes, for which it was given a very crudely made paint job for the imaginary "PAC Atlantic Air" line. The plane flew until 2000.

**Boeing 747-146**, 54th 747, serial number 19727, built in 1990. In 1996 Kalitta again made one of their old Jumbo-Jets available for filming. N703CK was also a former Japan Airlines plane, with JA8103 registration. It was chosen to play the title role in "Air Force One" with Harrison Ford. The famous U.S. presidential plane was imitated remarkably well when one considers that Hollywood's Air Force One was a much older version of the 747. By 2010 it is the only Lufthansa long-haul aircraft left in this livery.

**Boeing 747-123**, 136th 747, serial number 20390, built in 1971. This plane, which clearly shows its origins, was taken out of regular American Airlines service in 1974, since during the oil crisis the 747 proved too big for most routes. Shortly before it was rebuilt as a freighter it became the first 747 to play a major role in Hollywood in the catastrophe thriller "Airport 75." As the private jet of a multimillionaire played by James Stewart it sank in the ocean—naturally not really. This plane flew freight for UPS until 2008.

**Boeing 747-269B Combi**, 332nd 747, serial number 21541, built in 1978. Kalitta planes, specifically 747s, have played many leading roles in Hollywood movies. The ex-9K-ADA of Kuwait Airways still bore the blue-striped basic colors of that airline along with the fictional "Oceanic" title in the 1995 film "Executive Decision" with Halle Berry and Kurt Russell.

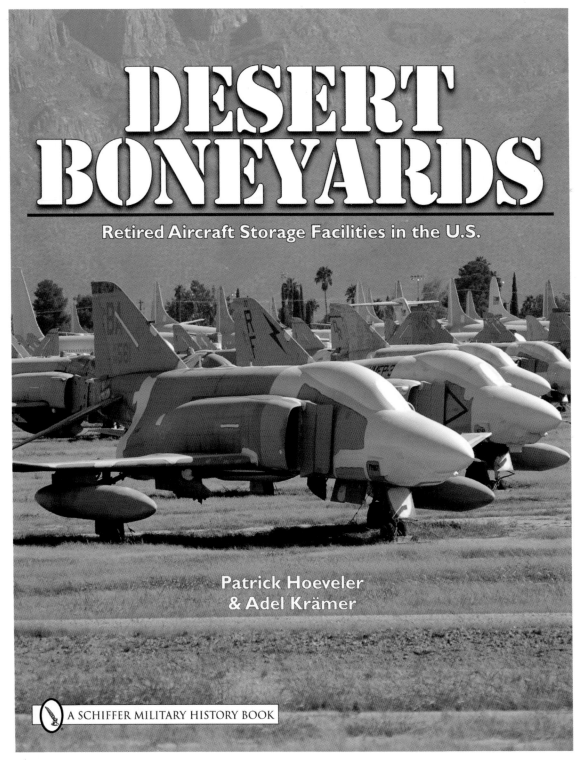

# DESERT BONEYARDS

Retired Aircraft Storage Facilities in the U.S.

**Patrick Hoeveler & Adel Krämer**

## DESERT BONEYARDS
## Retired Aircraft Storage Facilities in the U.S.
### Patrick Hoeveler & Adel Krämer

The "Desert Boneyards" are a concept well known to every aeronautical enthusiast, and yet also veiled in secrecy. Gigantic desert aerodromes in which military and civilian aircraft from all over the world are stored, either permanently or for a time, in order to serve as sources of spare parts or to be reactivated after a certain time. In this unique photo documentation, the reader is shown the best-known of these "desert boneyards" in Arizona and California and presented fascinating insights into a world far away from the well-known airports.

Size: 8 1/2" x 11"                     over 200 color images                     160 pp   hard cover
ISBN: 978-0-7643-3662-1                $45.00